MW01181018

The Cats, Max and Me

The Autobiography of a Cat-a-holic

Sharon Berry

www.wildberrybooks.com

Copyright© 2005 by Sharon Berry.
Printed in the United States. All rights reserved.

ISBN 1-58597-363-7

Library of Congress Control No. 2005908648

LEATHERS
PUBLISHING

A division of Squire Publishers, Inc.
4500 College Boulevard
Leawood, KS 66211
888.888.7696
www.leatherspublishing.com

# Acknowledgements

Hugs and kisses to my husband, Max, for believing in me and refusing to let me give up when I all I wanted to do was go to bed and pull the covers over my head. Thank you, Margaret McFarlin, my good friend and twin, for insisting I can write and for your contributions to this book. Thanks also, Bonnie Henson, for your input. Lots of love to Deborah Wattenberg for inspiring me to write this book, and to my many friends like Billie Burcham and Natalie Burns, who have stuck with me through the thick and the thin. To have good friends who do not judge but support is to be blessed. A big slurpy kiss to my friend and realtor, Mary Barickman, for moving us to a house large enough to comfortably accommodate our cats. A very special thank you to the Mission Animal Clinic for the excellent care they provide, for their kindness and for letting me pay on the installment plan.

For Domino
1990-2005

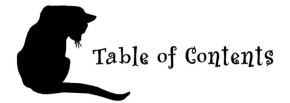

Table of Contents

Introduction

"My name is Sharon Berry and I am a cat-a-holic. I love cats; their smell, their touch, and their total disregard for my presence as they walk over me on the way to the food bowl. I love how peaceful and confident they are that they don't really need me to open the food cans. (They know how much I love to play with the can opener.) And I love the way they run through the house rearranging my furniture and breaking priceless antiques that I'm sure I would have thrown away, someday, when the newness wore off. Yes, I love my cats with all their idiosyncrasies. But, I especially love the way they know when I'm sad and rub against me to make me feel better. And, I love the way they will always be there for me whenever I need a little TLC. "

I'm not an expert on animals. I don't have a degree in catology and I don't claim to know the different breeds. Heck, half the time I can't tell how old they are or what sex. Oh, I've picked up a few tidbits here and there from the Discovery Channel. Like, cats sleep around 18 hours out of the 24 and there are 37 different species. But all that really matters to me is that one by one these fantastic creatures have shown up at my door looking for refuge and, in some cases, offering help. They came at a time in my life when I was at my lowest and have given so much more than I have ever given to them.

They came in all shapes and sizes; black, white, beige and calico, from kittens to chubby adults. There were wild cats, family cats and cats that came with street smarts. If a neighbor's cat wanted to live with me, I let him or her — inheriting three cats that way. The neighbors didn't mind. They seemed happy to be rid of them and I was happy to have them. Each came with its distinctive personality, each deciding that this was where they were supposed to live, that this was their home. I took them in, all of them. I became obsessed; the numbers didn't matter, they were welcomed at my door. I think they knew that I needed them.

In 1991 I found myself both physically and emotionally drained. For several years leading up to this point I'd been dealing with dental work that had gone wrong, severe hypoglycemia that resulted from not being able to eat properly, (if it didn't mush, I couldn't eat it), child abuse issues that surfaced, and menopause decided to set in just to make things more interesting. My doctor told me, "Let go. Go to bed." My body agreed, but my mind kept fighting it. I'd spent twenty years building a career in interior design and it was hard to walk away. How would I pick up the pieces when, or if, my life was given back to me? Finally, I found I couldn't go on anymore and with the devotion of my beloved husband, Max, I closed my business. We scaled down our lifestyle to the bare minimum, and I went to bed.

For the next two and a half years I contemplated my belly button and my role in the universe. Each day I'd cry till there were no more tears. I felt sorry for myself and threw a great big pity party for one. I felt like a failure and I kept thinking I should have been able to work things out. My doctor suggested I get into therapy to help me cope and soon my healing became a series of three steps forward, two steps back. There were days when I was too sick to get out of bed and didn't think I was going to make it. But, as many survivors of child abuse find out, we have an inner strength that refuses to give up.

While I was indulging in this self-pity a miraculous thing happened; I discovered life on a new level and animals started playing an important role in this discovery. I'd always had a cat or dog in my life but I never really knew those animals. Oh, I loved them, fed them, took trips to the vet when needed, but I never got deep down into their souls and let them into mine. They were ornaments in my life;

objects to amuse me and make me happy. But my view changed when I got sick. I learned there could be a lot of healing that comes from soft, furry creatures, especially cats.

These unique beings provided endless hours of comfort. Every night I have five to six sleeping on me, by me, under me. If I go to the bathroom one or more will escort me and when I return to bed I find someone has stolen the coveted "mama spot". I've gotten so used to them being there that I can't sleep without at least one drooling on me. Poor Max, so understanding, sleeping way over on the edge of his side of our king-size bed.

The cats have taken over as if it's their right. But I don't mind. I feel at peace with my babies surrounding me. It's as if I'm back in the womb, safe, and protected from the world. To each one that has crossed my path I say thank you. You gave me back my life.

# Chapter 1

Shadow, Domino Man and The China Doll

Before I would admit that I couldn't continue to function, three cats came into my life, two of which stayed with me through my healing. Through the one that didn't, I learned that cats have a sixth sense that lets them know when things aren't right, and how they're drawn to people they know will love and take care of them.

One day a beautiful charcoal gray cat started hanging around our house. I'd never seen him before and thought he was a stray or a new neighbor's cat. At first I ignored him, but each day he came back. Day after day he'd stand at the front door and demand food. I'd encourage him to go home, telling him I didn't need a cat, that I had a very nice dog named Muffy. But instead of leaving, he'd stretch himself out on the Oriental rug I had on our porch and close his eyes. He was having a sit-in. After several days of this I gave in and threw the poor guy a few table scraps. I again told him to go home, but of course he didn't listen. Sure, he was going to leave when someone is passing out free food.

I found out from a neighbor two doors down that his name was Dog and the bachelor who lived next-door to us had inherited him from his uncle who had inherited him from someone else. Seems he'd been abused by his first owner and neglected by his second. The bachelor was a rugby player and quite a partier and let the cat roam the neighborhood. Within a month of the cat's first appearance the bachelor moved. I heard the guy looked high and low for the cat, but he finally gave up and told my neighbor to tell me I could have the little runaway.

Of course, the minute the guy was gone the cat appeared. He sauntered into the house, jumped on a wingback chair and promptly fell asleep. Max named him Shadow. His wants were small and I, being the sucker of the world, obliged his every whim. In spite of his bad start in life he was a sweet, loving animal. With a little encouragement, he'd jump in bed with us Sunday mornings as we'd enjoy a leisurely breakfast in bed and read the Sunday paper. After weeks of painstaking patience I got him to take food from my mouth. Ok, I know, gross, but I enjoyed it. Shadow thought I was crazy but he'd do anything for a treat.

Being a street cat, every morning he used to make the rounds of the shops by our house. I didn't like Shadow roaming the streets but it was his life. The people knew him and fed him and I suppose they'd been doing this for some time. Once he agreed to live at our house I set forth some rules. He had to wait each morning till the traffic thinned before he could go begging and snooping and he had to return by 4:30, before the evening rush. Nevertheless, after two years of living with our new roomy, I made the fatal mistake of leaving him out one afternoon.

I'd gone to bed around 4:00 in the afternoon with a piercing migraine accompanied by nausea. I'd been having a lot of migraines during this period with terrible body pains and I was spending more and more time in bed. I was losing clients left and right and couldn't find the energy to look for new ones. Too sick to get up, and knowing that Shadow was a street cat, I figured he'd be all right, and he was, until Max came home around 5:30.

Max checked the cupboard for supper and, seeing that I was sick, decided to walk across the street to the grocery store. Shadow adored Max and many times accompanied him. This day, as always, he waited at the top of the metal stairs that led down from the bank parking

lot to the store for Max to come back. As Max and Shadow crossed the street to come back home, Shadow darted in front of a car. One minute they were standing on the curb waiting for the traffic to clear, the next, Shadow was lying in the street. Max was beside himself; he couldn't understand why Shadow would have done that. He knew better. He wasn't a kitten; he was at least three to four years old and had made that trip a hundred times before.

Max yelled for me to come quick and bring a towel. When I saw Shadow I knew he was dead, but hoped against hope that he was just unconscious. We rushed him to the vet and as I suspected, it was too late. The vet and staff were so comforting. One assistant put her arms around me and hugged me till my sobs softened. I could see the pain in all their eyes. It must be difficult to deal with death every day of your life. They calmed us as best they could, but what can be said in a situation like this? We took Shadow home and buried him under a lilac bush in the front yard so he could look out at the shops that he had so loved. I'm positive his spirit makes the rounds every day, visiting his friends, and looking for a handout. I hope I made a difference in his life. At least he died knowing he was finally loved; he was truly an amazing cat who never caused us any trouble.

Domino, on the other hand, was a handful. A black tuxedo cat with a white vest and four white paws, his face is all black with long white whiskers and sparkling golden eyes. He thinks I'm his mama and I've done nothing to discourage this notion. Of all the animals I've had, I have to say he is my favorite. He likes to lie in bed with me and snuggle under my left armpit. He'll look up at me with the most loving eyes and it's easy to see that he truly loves me as much as I love him, bringing me joy and a contentment I've never known before. He's quite a charmer in his tux looking like a little man.

I wasn't looking for a cat when Domi came into my life. I'd sworn off any more animals, forever. Shadow's sudden death left me shell shocked. I didn't want to ever feel that much pain again. So, when my son's wife, Tracey, showed up at my office one week later with this black and white kitten I said, "No way. I don't want any more cats. I have Muffy, thank you, and that's enough."

Tracey put the cat down on the floor and ran like hell out the door. Cursing and screaming I ran after her. I was still yelling as she drove away laughing her head off. I called my son to tell him what a cruel thing his wife had done, but I didn't get any sympathy. Kevin said they felt I needed another cat to help me cope with Shadow's death. I couldn't convince him I didn't want the cat. How could I make him understand I felt I'd let Shadow down, that I should have taken better care of him?

Domino was from a litter of wild cats that Tracey was trying to find homes for. The nursing home where she worked was by an open field and Domi's mother had given birth to several litters. This time the nurses decided they were going to catch the mama cat and have her spayed. They took her babies and found homes for them, with me as one of the chosen ones to receive this precious cargo; lucky me.

The first night of Domi's stay I put him in bed with me. He was so small and shook at the slightest sound. I didn't expect to get any sleep but thought by holding him I could get him to trust me and maybe get a little body rest in the meantime. During the night I drifted off for a few minutes and awoke with a start. There was something on my face. A little tongue was licking my mouth, kind of a "French Kiss" thing. Once I got my bearings I saw it was Domino and it was then that I realized he was doing to me what his mother must do to him. The poor little guy needed to be comforted. I kissed and licked his face like an animal would do and held him tight until he drifted off to sleep. He slid down my arm and positioned himself at my side. I sleep in T-shirts and Domi, still asleep, started sucking on my shirt right in the armpit. It seemed to comfort him so I let him do it. When I asked the vet about the sucking, he said Domino would stop it in about two years. "Two years? Are you crazy," I yelled? He never has; every night when I get in bed he's right there ready to "nurse."

I'd never had a wild cat before. Domi loved to fight and run

through the house at lightning speed. He was cute, precocious and always plotting his "Big Escape." The minute I'd open the back door to let Muffy out he'd shoot across the yard as far as he could before I could catch him, each time getting closer and closer to the fence that separated our backyard from the neighbors. As Domino's body grew larger and his legs stronger, he would run farther and farther until one day he made it to the fence.

He'd been planning this day for a long time, sitting on the back of the sofa in the upstairs sunroom looking out at the yard. His keen eyes had seen a hole under the fence, so hidden that Max and I didn't know it was there. This was his big chance to see the world. Just as his body slid under the fence I grabbed his leg. He tried to fight me, but I held on, determined that I knew what was best for him. After that attempt he gave up and it appeared he knew his fate was sealed. Domino Man was doomed to a life of hugs, kisses, ten meals a day, toys galore, and two weird, doting people that took his picture every time he tilted his head a different way. Or maybe he just realized he had a great gig.

To tame Domino's mean, savage ways I got a Siamese cat we named China Doll or "The Queen," as she quickly became known. I'd seen the movie *Lady and The Tramp* when I was a kid and remembered how mean those Siamese twin cats were and hoped China would be the same. She was a petite cat but had an aristocratic air about her. It was clear from the minute *she* decided to live with us that she wasn't taking any shit off anyone, period! China was the only cat I've ever paid for. She cost $25 at a local animal hospital and I'd convinced Max to buy her for my birthday. China took to her new surroundings well and as long as Domino stayed out of her way they got along. Instead, it was Muffy whom China singled out for attention. She would rub against Muffy's face and try to get her to love her and let her sleep against her body. Muffy would have none of it, politely moving away. China would repeat this process daily, with the same results each time, but she never gave up.

Unbeknownst to us, China was very ill when we adopted her. The

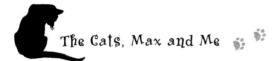

vet gave us antibiotics and we nursed her back to health. She hated taking her medicine and bit me each time I held her mouth open. After several bites my hands became infected but I was determined to save her life so I toughed it out.

Despite the fact that my own health was rapidly deteriorating, Max and I were happy and our pet world was complete. Animals add so much to our lives. As long as we have a soft creature to love we can shut the world out. It reminds me of a song written by Graham Nash of Crosby, Stills, Nash and Young fame:

"Our house is a very, very, very fine house
With two cats in the yard
Life used to be so hard
Now everything is easy 'cause of you." (© 1969 Giving Room Music)

Chapter 2

The Healing Cats

When I finally took my doctor's advice and went to bed, Max and I bought a hundred year old two-story farmhouse for me to heal in. It was small but had unique features, like high ceilings, fabulous molding and a gazebo attached to the end of our deck. We moved February 1, 1992 bringing with us Domino, China Doll and Muffy. I immediately started creating a charming setting for my big cure. Max painted several of the rooms to coordinate with the furniture we had, and I put my design skills to use, putting up draperies, and faux painting walls, furniture, anything I could get my hands on.

Trying to keep some sort of order to my day, I would get up each morning, put on makeup and wait, for what I didn't know; salvation, redemption? At 5:00 each evening I'd remove the cosmetic facade I'd constructed for the outside world to see and greet Max by 6:00. This lasted about a month. Finally, I let go and officially went to bed. No makeup, grubby clothes and a deep desire to get through this as quickly as possible. The child abuse issues seemed to be the dominant source of my problems, so I read every book on child abuse I could get my hands on and watched every TV show on child abuse — and there were plenty in 1992, from Oprah to Donahue. Everyone was speaking out.

A floodgate opened and everyone who had ever experienced sexual abuse as a child decided enough was enough. I felt like I had no control over what was happening to my life and, as more people spoke out, the more I felt like I was being outed. I only told a handful of friends and family what I was going through; I was too ashamed. To many of my acquaintances, I'd just dropped off the planet, and I wanted it that way. It was like I had fallen into a deep black hole and had to dig my way out. Once a week I saw my therapist, Barbara Hise, and tried not to go completely insane between sessions. She kept assuring me I wasn't crazy and told me all the feelings of hopelessness and despair I felt were part of the healing process.

One of the worst parts of the process was the body memories. As past traumas surfaced so did the physical pain. To deal with this I started seeing an acupuncturist. In 1989 I started doing alternative medicine [after seeing 29 mainstream doctors who all told me I was crazy.] The one doctor who believed me was Lee Veal. Lee was truly sent from heaven; he guided my healing in every aspect, from my diet to my mental state. By 1992 he felt he had done all he could for me and recommended an acupuncturist. Being stuck with needles all over my body didn't thrill me, but what the hell. I was so sick I'd try anything. Joseph Thomas was wonderful. I saw him for two and a half years; right up to the time I regained my life.

About the time I started seeing Joseph, my cat obsession began. On July 4th Max and I threw a party to both show off the house and celebrate the holiday. I hadn't seen anyone in months and needed to communicate with normal people. The party went well. Part of a homeless family, a mama cat and her baby I'd been feeding, made an appearance and entertained my guests. After our guests left the cats stayed and I decided to take them in. Several months later, I took in the papa. The mama was a beautiful calico with a hint of Persian and gorgeous eyes marked with black eye liner. She had been hanging around the house for several months looking for handouts when one day I noticed her nipples were enlarged and she'd lost some weight since the first time I'd seen her. I figured she must have had kittens. I asked several neighbors who the cat belonged to. I found out a single woman, Jeri, and her

three children who lived behind us had taken her in two years before. When I spoke with the woman, she told me the cat was content with them until their new baby arrived. The poor thing was put out because she was attacking the baby; I could have the cat if I wanted it. After all, it didn't really belong to her as she had taken it in as a stray. I asked about the kittens and she said she'd only seen one and guessed that's all there was.

Jeri called the cat Toby, but I renamed her Miss Priss. She seemed to like her new name better and always answered to it instead of that other name. Whenever I called her Toby her eyes got big and she looked frightened. She seemed to like my house and promptly made herself at home. I was worried how Domi and China would react, but it was obvious Priss had chosen this as her new home and no preexisting felines were going to sway her decision. Besides, she liked the steady flow of food that I always made available. From living on the streets she was always worried where her next meal was coming from, and to this day she can't get her tummy full and is at her food dish constantly. Anything will do, cat food or people food. It doesn't matter; she loves it all, especially sweets. Her craving for sugar is never-ending.

Priss is both a joy and a pain in the butt. An exceptionally loving feline who needs lots of attention, her favorite place to sleep is on my pillow. The minute Max or I sit down on the sofa she's on our laps — usually Max's chest. She plans these love-fests with Max right after dinner, when he tolerates them as long as he can before begging for relief. No matter how many times he puts her on the floor she jumps back up on him and continues for several minutes until I rescue him and make her sit on my lap. Nevertheless, she makes it clear what she wants, and the minute I set her on my lap she'll try to get back to Max. After several tugs-of-war she'll jump down and storm off in a huff.

Priss's kitten was a gray stripe that looked about two months old. I wasn't sure of her sex and thought she looked like a Skeeter. She wasn't afraid of me and was very appreciative at mealtime, so she decided to stay. Being so young, she adapted quite well to her new surroundings. Skeeter's not a very bright cat and sometimes I wonder how she would have made it in the world if I hadn't taken her in, but she has a special quality about her that is priceless. She feels what I am feeling; she knows when I am in pain and depressed and is there in an instant to do whatever she can to help me.

I was half out of my mind back then and had a terrible time sleeping. No matter how much I tried, I couldn't sleep; I felt too wound up. Skeeter sensed my anxiety and would paw at me until I'd lie down. Being so sick, I'd brush her away thinking she wanted attention, but soon it became evident that what she wanted was to give me attention. She would tuck her body into my neck and knead and knead until I relaxed and fell asleep. She did this both day and night over that two-and-a-half-year period that I spent in bed.

Sometimes I was a nonbeliever and thought she did this to comfort herself, but later I found out from Joseph that there's an acupressure point in that exact spot that, if stimulated, helps with sleeping. It's strange how Skeeter knew this. Does she have some sort of extrasensory perception? Do animals possess an instinct that lets them know when humans need them? I'll never know for sure, but I'm glad Skeeter has chosen to live with me. There have been many frustrating times in my life when she has suddenly appeared when I needed her most. Sometimes I seek out her help and other times she just appears in the middle of the night, always willing to tuck her body into the sleeping spot. She's such a sweetie; she always stays until I'm fast asleep.

When I took in Priss's mate, I found I had a second cat that possessed healing powers. Charlie was an orange tabby with a bad reputation for inflicting pain on both animals and humans. Charlie got his name because of a flyer I saw one day at the grocery store. A woman had lost her cat, Charlie, and the picture she had put up looked something like an orange tabby that was roaming my neighborhood. I called the woman and she came over and, as luck would have it, we couldn't find him. Max insisted it wasn't the same cat, but every time I called him Charlie he came running.

Through the neighborhood grapevine (children know everything that goes on in their neck of the woods) I found out that my Charlie had belonged to a family a block away. They said Charlie was the terror of the neighborhood and everyone, animal, child and adult alike was afraid of him. I was told he'd done extensive damage to another neighborhood cat. One girl claimed him as her cat and showed me a large hole and scars on the back of her leg. Her dad had put Charlie out on the street after that incident. She had called him Twinkie. Twinkie? No way. I called him that one day and he ran off.

At first I was afraid of Charlie, and after Miss Priss and Skeeter came inside to live, I'd find Charlie roaming outside crying for his family to come back. He'd peer in the back door and howl loudly. He started living full-time in the gazebo. Mornings when I went out to feed the birds and get the newspaper he'd come up to me and I'd run for the house. This went on for some time until one day I decided to try and make friends with him. At first I'd lay some food on the ground and run. After several days of that I decided to try to pet him. At first he tried to bite me and I was able to get away. But one day he got me good and as a reflex I hit him upside of the head with a plastic glass that had contained birdseed I'd just fed the birds with. He sat there stunned, shaking his head. I looked him in the eye and said, "There, that'll show you," and ran like hell for the house, my heart pounding the whole way.

Each day I left food out, but didn't try to touch him again. Then one day I thought, "This is silly, he's just a small animal," and I was determined to make him my friend. Again I tried to pet him and again he bit me. This time I purposely hit him upside the head with my plastic bird feeding glass. And slowly, triumphantly I walked to my front door. I looked back in time to see him shake his head in disbelief. That was the last time Charlie ever attacked me; after that he was proud to call me friend, and was grateful to see me whenever I ventured outside. He'd run up and rub himself against me, begging for food and to have his family back.

By winter I started letting Charlie come in the house for short visits. He'd roam around the first floor and periodically spray my furniture to let the other cats know he'd been there. I yelled at him to stop and after a couple of screaming fits he took to the rules of the house. It was obvious he wanted to be a part of this family.

One extremely cold, snowy night I brought him in and we both fell asleep on the sofa. When I woke up he was curled around me with his head tucked under my chin and his whole body wrapped around my chest. At that moment I knew he had to be mine. His little body was so comforting. For my Christmas present that year Max had Charlie neutered and he became part of the Berry clan.

Miss Priss wasn't happy to see him. She acted like she didn't like him, but once in a while I'd catch them nuzzling each other. Skeeter seemed oblivious to her dad and never gave him a thought either way. So much for family bonding. Domino and China were curious but gave him a wide berth when he entered a room. They weren't taking any chances.

Sometimes late at night I'd wake up and be in terrible pain with an excruciating migraine and I'd find Charlie sitting on top of my chest. He'd come up and sit real close to my face and spread his body across me. I'd try to get up to find an aspirin or something, knowing full well there wasn't anything that would stop the horrible pain in my head. Charlie wouldn't budge though. He would lay his head against my face and softly rub back and forth. I didn't ask him to, he just did it on his own. Despite the pain I was in I would then fall back to sleep and later, when I woke up, the pain was gone. I strongly believe that cat took my pain into his own body. I feel he had some instinctive healing device built into him. I also believe Charlie and his family came to me for a reason, as did Domino and China Doll. Without this group I would never have gotten well; of that I am sure.

During those years I spent in bed things took on a new meaning. I thought I had smelled the roses along the way, but until I stopped, stepped back and observed life from my bed I never realized what I was missing. I learned a lot about myself as well. Most of it I didn't like, but I did find I was stronger than I ever thought I could be.

Chapter 3

Do You Believe in Reincarnation?

I have had many occasions throughout my life to witness, first hand, that there is life after death and we should not discount things we cannot explain. When I was fifteen my father died, and for years after his death my mother, myself, as well as other family members and friends saw what appeared to be his ghost. Each of us described a tall, slender man with dark hair wearing a soft blue jacket. My father was the love of my mother's life and until her death at ninety she never got over him deserting us when I was six years old. She felt he regretted leaving us and stayed close to see that we were well.

I'm convinced there is a higher power and that things happen for reasons that aren't always clear at first. I have stuck with this philosophy throughout my life and when two outdoor male cats I had been feeding brought a small, gray, striped cat to my back door for food I set another place at the table. One cat I knew belonged to the neighbor who had originally owned Charlie. Neighbors told me his name was Dog but I called him Little Guy. He loved the name and would come running whenever I called for him. What's with these people who think it's funny to name their cats Dog?

Little Guy was black and white and rather slight of build. He'd obviously been in many scraps, as he had patches of fur torn away and several bad scars on his face, giving him a grisly appearance. He was only two or three years old, but carried himself like a cat that has been to three goat ropings and a county fair. I was outraged that my neighbor didn't take better care of him. I surmised the cat with him was a stray. I had scoured the neighborhood looking for an owner but no one ever claimed him. He was a rather nondescript, gray, plain looking fellow, but sweet-tempered. I'd been taking care of them, as well as many other wild cats for several months.

This particular cold, rainy day Little Guy and friend had what appeared to be a kitten with them. I instantly thought they were a family and called the gray cat Baby's MaMa and the kitten MaMa's Baby. Not very original, but I didn't feel very creative that day. MaMa's Baby was a shy, timid cutie that walked on her tiptoes and seemed to lead with her butt. She scarfed up the food I gave her and was soon sleeping on my deck regularly, and before long moved to the foot of my bed. When I used the bathroom at night she'd go with me and rub her tail against my legs and I'd stroke her body. Sometimes I'd grab her up and put her on my lap; she didn't like to be picked up, but I'd insist and she'd give in. This became a nightly ritual. She'd sit on my lap while I did my business.

Each time a new cat is brought into the fold, we always have it checked out to avoid infecting the rest of the herd but with MaMa's Baby I kept stalling. Although I knew we should've gotten her to the vet, we had one excuse after another. Many days I asked Max to drop her off and for some reason he wasn't able to. Each time I would be relieved and I'd get this strange feeling inside me, almost a premonition. I'd think, "Good. One more day I get to keep her." What a strange thing to think; where's that coming from? Still, I kept delaying the inevitable. I knew. Somehow I knew she wasn't here to stay and wanted to hold on to her for as long as I could.

During the third month we had MaMa's Baby, her breathing was labored and she couldn't seem to get enough air. She died shortly after the vet did emergency surgery. He told us it looked like a car had hit her at some time and all her insides had been shoved up under her

lungs. As she grew her lungs were cut off from the air she needed to live. He said she was pretty banged up and it was a miracle she had lived this long. Tremendous guilt set in. Could she have been saved if we'd brought her in sooner? The vet admitted he didn't know; maybe, maybe not, but he doubted it.

My grief was inconsolable. I'd never had this feeling before. Not for any human death that is. I felt like I'd let her down and lay in bed for days crying. I talked to my therapist but nothing helped. Then one day when I was grieving to the very depths of my soul I saw something that both scared and comforted me; a heart. Mine, and it was breaking. Right there in front of me, I swear it was my heart. In a deep consciousness, I had gone down so far I actually saw my broken heart. My body was tingling, my mind completely focused. There before me was this incredible sight. At the time I didn't know the meaning. I'm still not sure I do, I only know that a calm came over me and I knew that MaMa's Baby was coming back. I believe when MaMa's Baby died, I grieved so hard and wished for her return so strongly that she came back to me.

March was when this happened and I started counting. It takes what, three to four months for conception and birth, which meant she could be back by fall, at the very least. Every time I went outside I'd look for her, consumed with the thought that I would find her. This went on for months, during which time strange things started happening. One was so small that I'm sure most people would have me carted off to the looney bin for even bringing it up. I noticed on my cat calendar (is there any other kind?) on the June 1995 page, a picture of four cats: three adults and one kitten. Now, anyone who knows proper balance and design knows that everything is done in odd numbers, three, five, seven, etc. and, they never would have just stuck a kitten in a corner with three adults. The picture looked off, out of place. It was then that I knew for sure that MaMa's Baby was returning to me and would be back in June. Since the kitten in the picture appeared to have similar lines to MaMa's Baby, I took it as a sign.

On Saturday, June 13, Max called me from his recording studio to let me know there was a cat he thought I should take a look at. A male kitten had been hanging around for a few days and he and his staff had been feeding it. Even though Max thought it belonged at the house behind the studio, he still felt I should see it. I raced out the door, but he had already left for home by the time I made it there. Max was sitting on the sofa with this sweet little gray ball of fur curled up in his lap as I entered the front door. Carefully I sat down beside him and waited. MaMa's Baby and I had this special greeting; each morning as she lay at the foot of the bed I would bend over and rub my forehead against hers to say hi. We had done this every day, without fail, and I knew that if it were possible for her to come back she would greet me this way. If this cat was MaMa's Baby she would do this.

As I sat next to Max the kitten stood and crawled up on his chest. He (turns out it was a male) slowly walked across Max's chest to mine and came nose to nose with me, then stretched his little neck so his head touched my forehead, and rubbed. My heart stopped. I couldn't breathe. I sat there stunned, holding him for a few minutes. I needed more proof so I ran upstairs and grabbed a stuffed toy that I had bought MaMa's Baby. A yellow and white stuffed sock I had given her while she was still living on our deck, before I officially took her in, was her favorite toy; she would drag this toy everywhere. I placed it on the floor to see what the kitten would do. He jumped off the sofa and ran toward it. He recognized it and was glad to see it. Gently, I picked him up and ran upstairs, two at a time, set him in the middle of my bed and I laid down at the end. I had to see what would happen. He sat there looking all around the room, taking it in, seeming to recognize it. Could it just be wishful thinking? Suddenly, he saw a lace throw pillow that was propped against the larger pillows. He stared, did a little jump, raced over to it and looked at me. I grabbed him and started kissing all over his cute little face. It was MaMa's Baby, she had come back to me, I was sure of it.

Over the next few days it was obvious this cat had lived in this

house, with this set of people and felines. He knew the layout of the house and he knew the cats. Each time I've brought a new cat into the fold the existing guys have given the new one a hard time. There's always the get-acquainted period; the pecking order, the I've lived here longer and you walk three paces behind routine. But this time was different. Not one of them acted like he didn't belong, and Skeeter even took him under her wing, as she had done for MaMa's Baby, taking him to all the spots where she and Mama's Baby hung out, like her favorite behind the spare bedroom door. She set about playing mother. She groomed him, made sure he got to the food bowls on time, and acted as protector if a fight broke out.

BeBe, as we decided to call him, had other proof he was MaMa's Baby. Just like MaMa's Baby, he had a habit of walking sideways, leading with his tail. Other than that, he appeared healthy and happy and took to sleeping with me. BeBe was very interested in Domino's nightly ritual of nursing my armpit and decided he should have his own ritual of sucking my left earlobe. Thinking this was cute, I let him, until my ears started hurting so much I couldn't wear earrings anymore. I felt like I was having an allergic reaction. My doctor said BeBe's saliva contains acid or something that was eating away the protective layer of skin. I said "enough". So much for cute. No more nursing. Tee-shirts were one thing, skin was another.

Through the years BeBe has brought both comfort and joy to this household and his antics are legendary. At eight years, he likes to sleep on my pillow with his head tucked into my neck, which I let him do till the slobbers become too yucky. Quite large, he measures 33 inches, nose to tail, weighs over 20 pounds, and rules the roost. You had better move if he wants the chair you're in. He's conveniently forgotten how Skeeter mothered him and torments her between the love and kisses she bestows on him. He adores Max and loves to sit on his lap each night. His habit is to come up behind me and stand full height with his paws against my back to paw at my butt until I give him treats. Speaking of my butt, he used to bite it to get my attention.

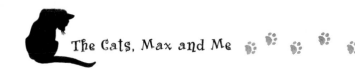

I put a stop to that real fast.

Lately, he has taken to sitting on my lap every morning when I visit the bathroom. He'll paw and paw at me till I let him up, and once there I have to stroke his head, kiss all over his face and tell him how much I love him. He eats it up. One morning I decided not to let him up as I was half asleep and not in the mood. Bad idea! With my eyes closed and drifting off I felt this heavy object draped across my back. BeBe had jumped on the back of the toilet, slid down and was resting all 300 pounds of dead weight across my back. His paws were on my shoulders with his head nestled into my neck slobbering. I laughed till I cried. Where's a camera when you need one?

Is it possible to return to this earth? Can a soul really come back? For me the answer is yes; I've seen it happen.

Chapter 4

Rosey Rosebud

Rosey is a strange creature who has a love/hate thing going with me. Her mother was another cat that Little Guy and Baby's Mama brought to me. For some reason I named the mother cat Sweet Pea. I don't know why. Who knows why we come up with the silly names for our pets? I'm sure there's some researcher out there who's done some incredible study at taxpayer's expense, but I haven't read it yet. Anyway, Sweet Pea was a wild cat that had little or no contact with humans and no intention of changing.

When I started feeding her she'd eagerly show up three times a day for meals and was getting friendlier and friendlier; then I made a horrible mistake. She was starting to take her meals inside with the rest of the brood, and one day I slid the sliding door closed. What a huge mistake; the poor little thing panicked. She was throwing herself against the glass door, running around the house, diving headfirst at the windows, rebuffing my attempts to soothe her. As she ran around the house, she was so frightened that she lost her bowels throughout. Finally I was able to guide her to the back door. When she made it out, the house was in shambles, the other cats were traumatized and I was confused. I hadn't expected that reaction from her. From then on, she and her brood kept a wide berth.

The following spring I helped Sweet Pea through the first of two litters. Precious, Domino II and Rosey Rosebud were born in the first litter. Precious was a beautiful female that looked a lot like Rosey, almost pure white. She grew to be gorgeous and healthy. Twoey, as I called him, was identical to Domino except his chin was white. He was an extraordinary creature.

Because she used to hide on the deck under this fabulous rose bush that had taken over the gazebo at the end of my deck, I'd given Rosey her name. The branches were so full of blossoms that they would rest on various parts of the wood and Rosey would peek out at me from under them. Pure white, with a charcoal tail, she had two patches of charcoal over each eye and was small and sickly. While the other two blossomed, Rosey grew listless and pale. Each day when I would put food out, the others would gobble it up, never giving Rosey a chance. She was so weak one afternoon I scooped her up, sat down on the deck steps and had a look. Sweat Pea went crazy, pacing back and forth, crying and howling.

Frightened and confused, Rosey looked up at me as I debated whether to keep her or give her back. I suspected Max would want to kill me if I brought another one in. I held her, loved on her and told her how beautiful she was, but in the end I put her down and walked away. I felt like a murderer. I knew she was sick and needed a vet, but was it my right to intervene? Shouldn't I let nature take its course?

Another month passed and I couldn't bear to watch that poor thing suffer anymore. I started plotting how I was going to get her. My first choice was for a sneak attack, but Sweet Pea, or one of the others, was always there to see that I kept my distance. Rosey hated me; I could see it in her eyes, and I couldn't get close enough. As far as she knew, her life was fine the way it was and she didn't want me to interfere. But I had to.

A time came when I just couldn't resist any longer. I snatched her up and ran inside. The cries were heartbreaking. I brought her to the door to show Sweet Pea she was all right, I wasn't going to hurt her. Rosey was covered with fleas and I knew I had to bathe her or the oth-

ers would become infested. I fed her, bathed her and told her how much I loved her and couldn't stand by and let her suffer. While I did this terrible deed I left the sliding door open a few inches so Sweet Pea could look in. As I was gently washing the fleas away a sound come out of Rosey's mouth that I had never heard before; a vibration from her vocals cords. I could feel them quiver and it got louder and more pitiful with each drop of water that touched her.

I felt torn about taking Rosey from the only family she had known. Does nature take care of it's own? Are some lives supposed to die to keep nature in balance? I don't know the answers; I just know it seemed like the right thing to do at the time. Unfortunately, I also knew Max would have a fit, and rightfully so, but I couldn't leave her out there to die could I?

So the saga of Rosey began. Of course I gave Max the usual spiel about finding her a home and that I could always put her back out when she was better. We both knew that wasn't going to happen; no one in the world could be trusted with such precious cargo, she was mine.

Taking the largest cat carrier we had, I made Rosey a house, placing signs I made with her name on them on the outside. Towels covered the floor and a flat Tupperware bowl became a litter box. Rosey was so small she could fit in the palm of my hand and in the beginning I didn't hold much hope that she would live. The vet took all sorts of tests, prescribed antibiotics and started the first of nine dewormings. Rosey had pneumonia. It was touch and go for several weeks. Each morning when I woke up I wasn't sure if I would find a dead cat in the carrier. Rosey must have had a very strong will to live; she never gave up.

She missed her mother so badly that it broke my heart and even though I would put the carrier at the back door so they could visit, Rosey knew she would never run free again. This sweet little cat has never grown to show me affection. I give her special treats; love her, on the rare occasion that I can grab her, and she stalks my every move. There are days I feel she must like me; she'll sit close, but not too close.

She sleeps on the foot of the bed so I can't stretch out, rubs against me at dinnertime, and will even let me pet her head, but she'll never do what the others do; show affection.

Chapter 5

The Condemned Cat Ate a Hearty Meal

In the summer of '97 Max had an opportunity to go out of town on business. I tagged along to lounge around the pool with a Mai Tai in one hand and a trash magazine in the other while Max worked. The only problem had been what to do with the kids? We'd had a kitty sitter in the past and she was very good. She came twice a day to feed them and clean their litter boxes; she even brought in our mail and watered plants both inside and out. Unfortunately, she had moved out of town and seeing as how we don't travel often we hadn't replaced her. We decided the next best thing for our gang was to board the entire brood at our vet. We had changed vets when we moved and the one we were using now seemed trustworthy.

Muffy, our chow, really liked them and when she needed shots or whatever would walk right in and head for the cage that was closest to the lobby and plop down. She considered it to be hers and refused to go to another. She liked being at the vet's so much that we would drop her off in the morning and pick her up at the end of the day. That way the vet had all day to take care of her needs and it gave her a day away from home. For her it was like being at a spa; she could interact with the customers, get treats and one of the employees would take her for long walks around the neighborhood. I left town feeling confident that everything would be fine.

On the day we came back I rushed the two blocks to see my babies. When I walked in I ran to the boarding area and took inventory. Everyone seemed okay. Domi cried, Priss ignored me as she was primping for the ride home, Rosey gave me her usual I-hate-your-guts look, but the others were happy to see me and ran to the edge of their cages, trying to get out. I had left instructions to bathe everyone on the day I was picking them up as I felt they would probably smell pretty bad after being caged up for a week. When I did a head count I was minus one; I found Charlie still in the grooming room getting his hair dried. He didn't look too happy so I had the assistant take him out. He was a little damp but otherwise ecstatic to see me.

After that stay, my beloved Charlie became listless and wouldn't eat like his usual self. Charlie had been sick for a three-year period with diarrhea and other ailments and now his diarrhea appeared to be getting worse. In the past he had seen a doctor on several occasions without the problem ever being determined. Charlie's original vet kept coming up with different reasons as to why he had diarrhea; one time he said Charlie had caught a parasite from a bird that he'd eaten, (trust me, Charlie would not eat a bird, yuck!) and put him on antibiotics. Another time the vet said we shouldn't give him store-bought food; he should only have Science Diet® or Iams®, which of course he sold. The list went on and on, all the while hinting we were bad parents. Our new vet suggested he run a battery of tests to find out what was wrong. Although Charlie had been tested upside and down in the past we gave him permission to do whatever he had to. We wanted Charlie well.

Max and I try to be responsible pet owners and always trust our veterinarians to do what needs to be done to protect our babies, so that's why we were in shock when we were told Charlie had feline leukemia. We stood there indignantly and said, "No he doesn't." We insisted Charlie's vet had tested and vaccinated him for feline leukemia. I didn't believe this doctor when he said the test came back positive and demanded a second opinion. Although the second test was negative we

were encouraged to have him tested again. We couldn't believe this was happening. Charlie had been given all the proper shots, or so we thought. We had the entire gang's medical records faxed to our new vet. Going back through these records he found that several of the cats had never been given the vaccine. We also discovered that several of them had been given the vaccine without testing. We were thrown into a nightmare. We had complete confidence this guy would always do the right thing for our pets. He had always stressed the importance of testing for leukemia; in fact he was phobic about it. He preached to me on more than one occasion about getting the cats tested, so that's why I was in shock.

At the urging of our new vet, we took Charlie to a specialist who tested him again with the results coming back positive. This latest vet said he wanted to test Charlie again in thirty days just to be sure, although both vets encouraged us to put Charlie to sleep immediately because they feared Charlie would infect the other cats. I couldn't; we couldn't. I put my head in the sand. Max, on the other hand, got on the Internet and pulled up every article he could find on feline leukemia. Given the inspiration I needed I rushed to the library, determined to beat this. What I found was music to our ears. Some cats do go into remission and can live up to 20 years with the feline virus. We prayed Charlie would be one of those cases and for months Charlie seemed fine. He ate, ran, and played as usual. There were no signs that he was in pain or discomfort. As a precaution, all the other cats were tested and given the vaccine every three months for a year. No one else ever came down with leukemia.

As the months passed my hope was shattered. I noticed Charlie hanging out at the water dish an awful lot and that his urine output was massive. At first I ignored it, and I chalked it up to too much water, but as it persisted I called the vet's office. They said it was part of the leukemia. I shrugged it off. Two more months went by and I noticed Charlie was having trouble walking with his back legs. Did he have a bladder infection or were his kidneys shutting down? I made an appointment with the vet. After several tests it was determined he had diabetes. I was given several options, but the most merciful, the vet said, was to let him go. I couldn't do it, not yet, I just couldn't. I needed more time; more time to show Charlie how much I loved him, how much I appreciated him being a part of my life. Every day was Charlie's birthday after that. He got loves and kisses till he begged for mercy.

Finally, we couldn't wait any longer. Charlie needed this to end. When he was diagnosed with leukemia he weighed 23 pounds; now he was down to 13. I had let Charlie have anything he wanted to eat trying to keep his weight up. It wasn't easy because in the back of my mind I kept thinking, "Oh no, he can't have that! It'll make him sick," but what did it matter? Nothing I did helped. Charlie was dying and I couldn't stop it.

The weather was cold and threats of snow were on the weatherman's lips that fateful day. At 7:30 a.m. I opened a can of Fancy Feast® beef cat food and a can of their chicken chunks. No bland food today. I was amazed at how much he ate. He gobbled his food like the pig he is and even stole off the other cats' plates. Let him. What would be the harm?

At 8:30 a.m. I sat down and took Charlie in my arms. I could tell he knew something wasn't right about today. I hugged him and kissed all over his face then looked deeply into his eyes; those wonderful gold eyes that were now fixed in a permanent stare. How to tell him within one hour he would be dead. How could I make him understand this was for his own good? Was I right, or was I being selfish because I couldn't bear to see him suffer anymore? What if the doctors were wrong and he wasn't sick at all? What if they'd lied to me? Would they do that? For what purpose?

Max got the cat carrier but I said no, I'll carry Charlie. Starting toward the door, I put his leash on. He jumped from my arms and ran upstairs. Running after him I kept thinking, "He knows. He's trying to tell me he wants to live! Should I let him?" Gently carrying him outside, I let him walk on the grass. Again, he tried to run away. Was I doing the right thing? I finally got him in the car. The vet is only 10 minutes from our house but the drive was an eternity. Charlie kept looking in my face and crying. He was begging for his life. My guilt was overwhelming and I thought I was going to throw up. At 9:36 a.m. my beloved Charlie drew his last breath; nineteen months after being diagnosed with leukemia, six years after joining our family.

Although I love my cats, each and every one of them, Charlie touched my heart like no other. I will be eternally grateful for him and the love he brought to my home. I hope I did the right thing by showing him mercy and letting go. God knows it was one of the most difficult decisions I've ever had to make. I owe that cat so much. I owe him my life. He will be sorely missed. Goodbye my love. Goodbye Charlie. I love you.

For days after Charlie's passing, the pain seared to my very inner being. My heart was crying; I didn't know how I would be able to stand it. I lay in bed screaming, "Come back Charlie, come back. Don't leave me. I need you. Please forgive me." How would I ever make it without my beloved? Every time I went to the front door I envisioned him there asking to go out. He used to say "out", and since I did not want him to go out I would pretend I thought he meant food and would give him treats to pacify him. As a result, he was a blimp. Max had several nicknames for him; "Tubster" was his favorite.

I have many fond memories of Charlie. My life was definitely better for having him in it. But it hurts like hell that he will no longer be there in the middle of the night when I need him. I'll never again see him chase Miss Priss up the stairs or hear those pitiful little cries when his feelings are hurt. I miss his morning greetings when I'd bend down and kiss his nose and then he would kiss mine. The house is full of reminders that once a mighty warrior lived here. Max said Charlie had climbed up on the sofa a few nights before his passing and sat really close to him, putting his head on Max's leg. He hadn't done that for a long time; he hadn't done a lot of things for a long time. I forgot that he didn't interact much anymore. He was always asleep in the kitchen

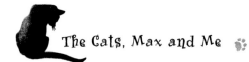
with his head resting on one of the water bowls. Sometimes I would see him in his spot on the stairs. Every morning I'd have to climb over him on my way down to the kitchen. He wouldn't budge an inch and I couldn't move him even with my foot. It was either step on him or over him. Sometimes it would be his tail I'd step on. He'd let out a yelp, but he still wouldn't move; not until he'd hear that can opener, then he'd come a-runnin', hell bent for leather, the first in line. That was my Charlie.

Chapter 6

Salem the Talking Cat

The third cat I inherited from the neighbors was a black male that reminded me of the cat "Salem" on the hit TV show *Sabrina, the Teenage Witch*. Our Salem showed up on our doorstep with a puncture in his left shoulder. Pure black, including his whiskers, his eyes were a soft gold with the weight of the world showing in them. Although he was bleeding, he immediately started telling me his story in great detail. He was quite frightened and it was obvious he needed a place to hide. I took him to the vet to have his wound cleaned and asked about the cause of the injury. The vet said an animal could have bitten him, but the wound was perfectly round and looked to me like someone had burned him with a cigarette. The vet didn't think so but I wasn't convinced an animal could make that perfect a bite without leaving a rip or tear.

I let Salem set up housekeeping in my gazebo and brought him food and water thinking he'd go home and I would be spared the duty of informing Max we had a new roommate. Just in case I was wrong about the abuse I tried to find Salem's owner. I didn't have any luck. About two weeks later I saw one of the children who had owned Charlie. I told the boy about a black cat that was living in my gazebo and asked him to take a look in case he knew who Salem belonged to. Wrong move. It turned out Salem was his cat, and the minute Salem saw him he took off. The boy ran after him, but Salem gave him the slip.

Day after day the boy kept coming back trying to retrieve Salem, but Salem always got away. One day the boy told me his father said Salem only hung out at my house because I fed him. He then sat down and told me a loving story about how his father had built a special seat for Salem's mama so she could watch television. I thought okay, maybe I'm way off base here, and in a weak moment I plotted to capture Salem and turn him over. The boy said Salem was escaping through a window in their living room and promised it would be fixed. Reluctantly, I caught Salem and put him in the boy's arms.

The next morning at 6:00 a.m. I went outside to get the newspaper and saw Salem casually walking up the street. He'd already passed my house and I can only assume he was on his way to friendlier territory. When I called his name, he came running in leaps and bounds, ran into the house and has never been out since. "He doesn't want to go," I told the boy point blank when he came looking for his cat. I expected a fight with the father but none came, and soon after they moved. The boy stopped by one day and told me his dad said I could have Salem, and the mama too if I wanted her. I gave a pass on the mama.

While Salem was living in the gazebo we'd have daily chats about his world. He'd share with me the places he'd gone, the things he'd seen. He'd tell me about the opossum that came on my porch at night to eat the sunflower seeds, and talked about how the raccoons washed their food in the water I always left out. I listened in awe, and after he'd tire of talking he'd curl up in my lap and fall asleep. Knowing he could let down his guard for just a little while he'd let out a big sigh. But once inside, Salem never said another word. No matter how hard I tried to get him to engage in a conversation he refused to say a thing, not so much as a meow, until December 22, 2003. Salem was having problems with his bowels and was constipated. Each morning and evening I watched as he struggled to get just the smallest turd out.

The vet said to give him pumpkin from the can, the pure kind with no spices. At first Salem gobbled it up when I mixed it in with his food. A new taste treat, yummy! The thrill wore off after the first few days and he wouldn't touch it. For two weeks I mixed pumpkin with all kinds of food to get him to eat it. "Nope, you can't make me," he seemed to say.

I tried everything to get him to go regularly. I even consulted my Natural Health book on cats and tried physillium husk, just like it said. Each morning and evening I'd sprinkle finely grated physillium husk on his wet food. This seemed easier to disguise and Salem ate it. But he still wasn't dumping more than a small stool. Once, though I actually saw him really go. I mean a full-blown dump. I was jumping for joy. "Salem had a shit, Salem had a shit! Good Salem." He was so pleased with himself he grinned from ear to ear. It looked like a normal bowel movement, just like the other cats had. But alas, this didn't last, and no matter how much physillium or pumpkin I tried he just couldn't go. I finally decided to take him to the vet.

I had Max get the carrier and hide it in the laundry room on his way to work. No point in alerting everyone. I've had too many runs around the house with these guys. Why are they so afraid? It's just a ride in a big foreign object that makes all kinds of strange noises with the destination a strange place filled with barking dogs, weird people looking in the carrier saying unrecognizable things, and finally sitting on a cold table with a grumpy man poking and prodding their bodies and doing unspeakable acts. Why should they hate that?

Once in the car Salem started to whimper and then he started talking. I couldn't believe my ears and waited to see if he'd say it again. He did. He said "how-ee-a" over and over. I started saying it back to him, all the while reassuring him he'd be all right, but he kept saying "how-ee-a" louder and louder. I tried to understand him, but he sounded like my three-year old niece, Briann, whose words come out jumbled and undecipherable, but she is definitely telling me something. Only her mother and father can understand that language. I should ask my niece what he was trying to say.

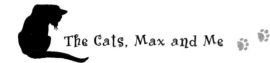
The vet checked Salem inside and outside, upside and downside. Nothing. He took two x-rays that only revealed a large stool ready to come out.

Hallelujah! Hallelujah! Salem had a bowel movement. It took two enemas, and his own litter box, but he finally went. The food he's eating is high in fiber and should be cleaning him out, according to the vet, but as it isn't, he gave me a laxative and said to keep giving him physillium as well. The poor little guy. I only hope he doesn't over go, like my poor 88-year-old mother, who can't control her bowels and goes constantly. The minute she eats it goes right through her.

Chapter 7

Once a Thief...

I had a dream last night that one of my cats levitated. A silly dream really. Weenie was wearing goggles like pilots do, only these were clear and so large they wrapped all the way around his head, with clear straps that crisscrossed his chest. He seemed perfectly content floating about eight inches off the ground. I can't for the life of me figure out what the significance of that dream was.

Little One and Weenie are brothers; their big sister is Rose. They're from the second litter of Sweet Pea. Have I confused you yet? I hadn't intended to keep either one. I fed the outdoor troops one night in October of 1997; Sweet Pea, Little Guy, Baby's Mama and Sweet Pea's newest offspring. Five this time. Little One, as I came to call him, was four weeks old when he ventured in our back door and made himself at home. A gray-striped, fearless cutie, he wandered throughout the kitchen checking out every corner and standing up to the other indoor cats if they got too close. He wasn't at all afraid.

After everyone had eaten I put Little One on the deck and started to close the sliding glass door. He ran like the devil back inside. I cuddled him and thought how cute and put him out. He ran for all he was worth back inside just before the door closed. Knowing that Max would kill me if I brought another one in, I put him out again. He came back. I called Max and told him what was going on and promised I'd find him a home. It was obvious he didn't want to live on the streets. Sweet Pea was freaking. I didn't know what to do; she already hated me for taking Rose and now to steal another one? How could I do this to her? Let's see, living in storm drains or a comfy, cozy bed. My family grew to eight.

A week later I snatched one of the black kittens and tried and missed for the other black one. I never could get him. From my work at the Metropolitan Organization to Counter Sexual Assault (MOCSA), I'd learned that Halloween and black cats were a breeding ground for torture. We named this one Halloween after deciding against Indigo. He was pure black but it soon became obvious Weenie was to be his name.

There was someone who was going to adopt Weenie but not for two weeks. Bad move. I told Max I wouldn't be able to part with him if I kept him that long. The girl changed her mind and my family grew to nine.

Little One and Weenie are the nuttiest, craziest pair I've ever encountered, more entertaining than television. Max agrees. Their antics are legendary and they tumble, fight and amuse 'round the clock. Little One is more loving while Weenie is schizoid; he loves, but on his terms. Not in an uppity cat way, but a frightened, not quite sure I can trust you way. I'm sure Rosey has something to do with that. I believe the three of them must know they're from the same mother as they have a special bond. Sometimes I feel like Rosie conspires with Weenie against me. Paranoid, you say?

Little One has the personality and interacts with us the most. He loves to sleep on my chest, legs, or stomach and no matter where I am he makes himself at home. As with the rest of the troops we've developed little pet names. Little One's is "Cutie Patootie" or "Mr. Patootie" as he likes to be called, while Weenie is "Weiner schnitzel."

The cats had the usual round of tests and shots when we brought them in, along with regular checkups, but these two have never been sick a day in their life. Weenie had something wrong with his eye once

and even though the doctor gave him antibiotics, he couldn't even be sure it was an infection. He thought maybe he'd just gotten something in that eye that irritated it. It was totally baffling when, in June of 2003, Little One didn't come for breakfast. If the kids don't eat it's time to call for an ambulance. No amount of coaxing could get Little One downstairs for his morning feast. I climbed the stairs and decided to serve him breakfast in bed. He wouldn't eat so I brought him treats. Now, if they don't eat treats it's time for the undertaker.

I whisked Little One off to the vet, who ran a full set of tests and checked him from head to toe. He started in with the guilt trip, making me think I neglected the poor guy. He felt it was AIDS or leukemia and since Priss was diagnosed with AIDS in 2001 he felt Little One probably caught it. I've never been convinced that Priss has AIDS; one test said maybe while the other said no. I decided to take a wait-and-see approach.

I did challenge the vet on the leukemia diagnosis. Since all my guys had been tested and given multiple shots of the leukemia serum, I told him to look further. The tests came back negative on both conditions. Little One's white blood cell count was registering 32,400 when normal was 16,000-18,000. Additional test results wouldn't be in until the next day so they started him on antibiotics. It was a long night. Within 24 hours Little One was 80 percent better, not all the way back but enough to eat and hit Salem up side the head. Finally the vet called and said they couldn't find any infection but he tested positive for Toxoplasmosis that had nothing to do with what was going on in his body now, although it needed to be treated. They were going to continue to monitor his white count.

The only thing I knew about Toxoplasmosis is that pregnant women shouldn't change the litter box because they might catch it. The vet gave me an overview of the disease, an infection by the intracellular parasite Toxoplasmosis gondii. The parasite can infect nearly all species of warm-bloodied mammals, including people, while cats are the definitive hosts for this parasite. The brain, heart, liver, intestines, eyes, adrenal glands, and muscles can all be infected.

Little One wasn't having any of the symptoms of Toxoplasmosis and the vet thought he'd had it a very long time; probably got it from his mother. With antibiotics for his infection and Clindamycin® for the Toxoplasmosis, I had my hands full administering both twice a day; the antibiotic for two weeks and the Clindamycin® for one month.

After the first week they checked his blood and urine and decided to go another two weeks with the antibiotic. His white count was down to 19,000 and he was on the road to recovery. In the beginning he took his medicine like a brave little soldier, but by the second week he fought me tooth and nail. After each test of wills Little One would come up to me and rub against my leg as if he knew I was just trying to help him. I'd kiss his face and let him know I loved him.

Just as fast as the symptoms came, they were gone. Little One was back to his old ornery, sweet self; running a million miles an hour, tormenting Priss and Skeeter and collapsing in my lap for hours until I couldn't hold my water any longer. Ahh, the joys of motherhood.

Chapter 8

And Back to Nine

China died in 1998. I came home one day and she was curled up in front of the sliding glass door in the kitchen. Her eyes had a dazed, contented look and I thought she was asleep. She was in the sunspot, all cozy and relaxed when I tried to wake her for dinner, but she ignored me. Finally, I went over, touched her and found her body was stiff. She had obviously died earlier in the day. How horrible for the other cats; I wondered how many times they went to her trying to help or wake her?

The vet's office told me to bring her in. I gently wrapped her in a soft, pink bath towel. She was covered in ants and I tried to pick them off. In the car, with China lying on the seat next to me, I remember thinking this would be the last time I would ever be with her. An empty feeling of dread washed over me and I thought I was going to vomit.

An autopsy was done but nothing was found. Because of a bruised spot on her lip, they suggested she'd been electrocuted. "That's ludicrous," I told them. Her fur wasn't singed; there weren't any burn marks. No way had she come in contact with electricity, there aren't any cords on the kitchen floor. She would have had to bite a cord in my office, two rooms away, and then walk all the way to the back door in the kitchen.

Could a spider have bitten her? They weren't sure. There were no toxins or poisons in her system and although they could do further testing the vet didn't feel it would reveal anything new. China had been sickly and infected when we first got her, I asked if maybe she had a bad heart? He just shook his head and scrunched his shoulders. I guess we'll never know.

I had a hard time going back to the house without her. The cats were all lined up waiting for me when I walked in the door. I just looked at them with my tear-stained face and one by one they went about their business. Domi jumped on the sofa beside me and curled up in my lap. After awhile I lay down and drew his body close to mine. We stayed that way for what seemed an eternity, sharing our grief.

How strange to miss China, who didn't interact all that much but was such a presence that life revolved around her when she walked in a room. China was the queen and this house was her kingdom. We were all her faithful subjects, especially Domino. He misses her the most. She was his mate, his better half that slapped him up side the head when he didn't respond fast enough to her wants. She kept him in line. Now he looks confused and lonely.

China loved to sleep on top of my computer monitor while I worked. I was forever moving her tail or a paw out of my way to see the screen. She'd go limp and doze off while my fingers clicked across the keyboard. Sometimes I'd have to catch her when she stretched too far. This spot was her favorite. The heat from the monitor kept her bottom warm while the rays of sunshine that streamed in through the window warmed her top. She was in heaven.

Other preferred spots included the ledge in the bathroom next to my office; she'd jump up there and taunt the others to get her. No one else has ever been able to figure out how to get up there. I've shown them a million times. First you jump on the sink counter top and then up to the ledge. But, no, they just don't get it. China liked any place high, the higher the better. I miss the "Queen." Long live the Queen!

It took two years before my feline life became balanced again. Then one day a special creature walked into my yard. At first I ignored his pitiful cries, since I was on my way to work and, as usual, was late. He was sitting under my willow tree as I was getting in my car, a beautiful orange and white tabby, fluffy and healthy looking. He was rather skinny, but not everyone stuffs their animals till they waddle. He looked sad and confused and reminded me of Charlie. Could it be? No, I figured he was a neighbor's cat. None of my business, got to go! Bye! He kept crying, as if he needed help, and I figured he probably wanted a handout, so I ran in the house and got him a handful of treats. There, I'd done my part. See ya!

Two days later he was back and begging for more. This went on for several days and although I knew I shouldn't encourage him, I just couldn't help myself. I always try to resist, but then give in. Why me, Lord? Why do they always come to me? Before long he took up residence under our porch, making himself right at home and acting as if he were part of the family. I kept thinking he would go home, but he never did. Surely he must belong to someone, but as with every cat before him, no one came looking.

A woodchuck had been hanging around, eating the sunflower seeds we leave for the squirrels. He too had been seen under the porch but Max was afraid he'd hurt the cat, so we took the poor little homeless waif in. Max thought he must have belonged to a neighbor who moved two weeks before, but I couldn't believe someone would just move away and leave him. Who knows what people will do though.

It wasn't long before Baby Huey, as we named him, was a little porker. He was the most loving creature on earth who liked to be petted and groomed and kissed, with tummy rubs his favorite thing. I started calling him my chubby tummy tel-e-tubby. He would throw himself down and lie on his back with his paws all curled up looking up at me so cute. I couldn't resist. Throwing myself on the floor, I'd rub and kiss his tummy till he begged for mercy.

As with all the cats we've taken in, Huey went to the vet for a thorough checkup. He had this strange way of holding his mouth and we discovered one of his fangs was gone. We showed this to the

vet, who thought he'd been in a fight. Of course, with my wild imag-
ination I had envisioned his owner kicking him in the mouth and
throwing him out on the streets. We were advised by Dr. Erickson,
with the Mission Animal Clinic, to have the other fang pulled, too,
since it was cracked and probably giving him problems.

The results of the tests came in and showed the source of the constant crying for tummy rubs was worms. So, Huey was de-wormed,
tested and given shots for every disease imaginable, and had his fang
pulled. After the big cure Huey wasn't so receptive to his tummy being
rubbed. He didn't need me now and I was crushed. My baby had
grown up. Now all he cared about was FOOD!

Huey is on a mission to eat every morsel out there. When I set the
food dishes down, he has this bad habit of eating Domino's food.
Huey is always fed first in an attempt to get him to leave the others'
food alone, but the minute Domi's dish goes down, Huey is there to
scarf it up. Domi is pushed out of the way and Huey starts to gobble.
I yell at him, but mostly Domi resigns himself that Huey is a jerk and
moves to another dish.

In the morning, Huey loves to go out with Max to get the morning
paper. He loves to sit on the porch and watch me walk across the street
to the mailbox and loves rolling on the sidewalk in the sun. Never
once has he tried to leave the yard, and when I go too far or am out of
sight, he panics and is at the door waiting to get in when I return.

Huey has never once tried to run away, which is pretty amazing. I
found out he originally lived only six doors down from me. The
neighbor across the street came over one day to talk and recognized
Huey. She and another neighbor had taken care of him and she was
sure he was the cat that lived at the end of my block. When he stopped
coming around looking for food, she feared he'd been killed. What a
relief to see he'd found a new home and she could share this news
with her friend. She couldn't get over how fat he was. I told her all the
things we'd had done to get him in shape.

I was terrified she would tell his owners, but she said they didn't deserve him. They had never looked for him or given him another thought, according to her. I felt my secret was safe. Am I a bad person? Why is it I feel no one can be trusted with these special creatures but me?

Chapter 9

Skeeter's Big C

In early August 2003 I discovered a lump on Skeeter's stomach. We had just finished dealing with Little One's illness when I noticed Skeeter holding her mouth oddly, the way Huey does. When I looked in her mouth her left fang was gone. Shocked, I held her, rubbing her head and eventually her stomach. It was then I felt the lump.

Exhausted from Little One, I didn't know if I could go through another illness so soon. I knew the lump wouldn't go away, but decided to sit on it for a few days. Plus, being short of cash, I didn't have any other option; without a steady paycheck in two years and Max's business barely hanging on, we waited. After two weeks I felt the lump getting bigger and decided to take action. Since I had some room left on a credit card, I made the appointment — luckily, everyone takes plastic. My poor healing cat, I couldn't let anything happen to her. A faithful companion for twelve years; it was now my turn to give back.

The doctor examined Skeet on Friday, August 22 and scheduled surgery for the following Monday morning. No food after 8:00 p.m. and take her water away in the morning.

The weekend was a long one trying not to worry, but emotions took over. Looking back over the years she's been with me and how long she's been there to comfort me, I didn't know if I'd be able to go on without her. When I can't sleep at night and the pain is unbearable she's there to reassure me. She tucks her body against mine and starts those paws a-kneadin'. She won't let up no matter how much I protest. Sometimes she's just downright too hard, but on she goes until I release and rest. It's as if she knows what's best for me.

Neither Skeet nor I got much sleep that night. All night I loved and kissed on her, and come morning she was in heaven. Trusting. I had Max drop her off at the vet's at 8:00. The frightened look on her face and the questioning eyes as to why she was left behind was more than I could bear. Her first visit was uneventful; no shots, just a quick exam, with lots of love and treats. But how could I look into those sad eyes and see the realization of betrayal. If only we could communicate with our pets; tell her this is for her own good, that I loved her and wanted her to live and without the surgery she would die. My poor, sweet Skeet.

Before Max could get back home the vet's office called with questions. Did we want pre-blood work? Yes. "That was already okayed," I told her. "They have her down for dental, is that correct?" she questioned. "What does that entail?" I asked. "Seventy dollars to clean her teeth? No," I said. Although a fang was gone, the doctor thought there might be pieces still there. I had already authorized him to take any debris out. I reminded her of this; she said they knew.

I had asked Max to tell them to call me the minute she was out of surgery. Not trusting anyone, I reminded her to call the minute they knew anything. By 11:00 I hadn't heard anything and called them. The girl who answered wasn't too helpful, other than Skeet was in surgery now. My heart was pounding and all I could do was pray. "Please God don't let anything happen to my dear, sweet little girl," I pleaded.

My heart skipped a beat at 11:06 a.m. when the doctor called. She was doing fine. He was through with the lump part but wanted to talk to me about her teeth. He couldn't find anything left of the fang that fell out, but he did find another tooth that needed to be pulled. Giving him permission to do whatever he needed to I thought how strange, that when we're in panic mode we'll OK anything, no matter what the

cost. I'll find a way to pay I thought; Skeet's health comes first.

More stress. 11:13, 11:27, 12:00, with still no word. My head was starting to hurt. At 12:14 the phone rang. It was my mother. By 1:00 I decided they weren't going to call, that they probably figured they had already let me know what was going on. I'll call later.

At 4:01 I called the vet to see when I could pick up Skeeter. The girl told me 5:00, so at 5:00 I pulled into the parking lot. Poor Skeeter. She could barely stand up but was very happy to see me. The doctor cleaned her up some more, gave me instructions and we were on our way. Her spirits picked up a little as she recognized the car. When we reached the house I opened the rear door and let her see we were home. She was so excited.

I brought Skeeter upstairs in her carrier and made a bed for her on the floor next to my bed, thinking she'd find comfort in being by me. Once I opened the carrier door she cautiously came out and immediately fell as she tried to get on the bed. Gently, I picked her up and laid her down. Being pretty groggy, she tried to walk but kept slipping. It appeared she couldn't get comfortable. She'd sit for a while in one spot then move to another. Stroking her head, I kept telling her how much I loved her and how sorry I was for her pain. She looked at me with such sad eyes one moment and then those pitiful eyes would turn to hate. She definitely was mad at me and she wanted me to know it was going to take a long time for her to get over this.

Leaving her lying on the bed I went downstairs to start Max's dinner and called my mother and Max to let them know Skeeter was home. The rest of the troops were begging for food, but I ignored them. They were not eating tonight. The doctor had said Skeeter could not have food until morning. He was afraid she'd throw up. She could have water in a few hours though. The minute I walked in the kitchen I picked up the cats' food and water dishes. I was afraid Skeet would come down and surprise me. I didn't need to wait long before there she was. Even though she still couldn't walk a straight line, Skeeter insisted on staging a sit-in. Her body language made it clear she wasn't moving until she'd eaten. The kids gathered round smelling and grooming her so I let them comfort her a bit and then decided to take her back upstairs. I hated to have her even more mad at me but I picked her up anyway. She was angry and fighting me all the way. Holding her tight, I put her in the carrier. I felt better knowing she wasn't going to fall down any stairs.

After dinner Max and I went up to sit with her. We put her on the bed and kept letting her know we were there for her. At 8:00 p.m. I gave her water, but she didn't want any. I took her to the litter box. Nope. She shot downstairs for the kitchen and did another sit-in. It's going to be a long night.

On my lap, on the living room floor, to the kitchen, upstairs, downstairs, round and round she went. At 10:00 p.m. she finally drank some water. She refused to come upstairs at this point and lay down in the kitchen. During the night she snuck into bed beside me and at 5:30 I found her sitting in the upstairs hall. After I petted her head a few times, she acted like she wanted to use the litter box so I cleaned one out. She smelled it, no, not this one. She went to another. I cleaned it with the same results. Off she went. When I came downstairs at 6:30 I couldn't find her. At 8:00 she was still missing. I fixed breakfast and went looking for her. She was under my bed, so I pushed the plate of food under there for her. Since she looked interested, I slowly moved away. Thirty minutes later I checked and found she'd eaten just a little off the top. Skeet was gone again and I figured she'd dug in even deeper. My first instinct was to hunt her down and force her to come out, but then I decided to leave her alone. She'd been through so much. She wasn't used to this kind of abuse.

At lunchtime I was able to entice her out with Science Diet® Savory Cuts, filled with soft chunks of meat and gravy. She licked all the gravy and was able to manage a few of the chunks. Glad she had an appetite, I ran downstairs and got her some milk; she drank almost the whole bowl. Now she's on the mend.

Over the next two days she slept, ate and slept some more. The

doctor said it would take a few days for the results of the tests to come through to determine if she had cancer; all we could do was wait and pray.

When Dr. Erickson called I was totally unprepared for his words. Although he got the entire tumor, tests revealed that Skeeter had cancer cells that can form more cancer and he recommended doing radical surgery. He wants to take everything on her left side and do chemo. Malignant chemo, radical wider margin, take everything on that side. My brain is fogging up; nothing he says is registering. I can't think. I never dreamed this would be the result. She would be OK and we would go about our business, she being cute and loving, and me giving her tons of love, treats and playtime. Pets aren't supposed to have human illnesses.

Max said let's wait and get more info before we make a decision. By Friday I still couldn't deal with it and decided to wait for her appointment next Thursday when they remove the stitches. Putting my head in the sand, I pushed away all thoughts of her dying.

Skeeter's appointment to remove the stitches was September 4. Dr. Erickson wasn't available that day so Dr. Brown saw us. He said the wound looked good and it was healing nicely. We discussed the cancer and I told him Max and I were not ready to put Skeeter through intense surgery, followed by extensive chemo. Dr. Erickson had recommended a specialist and Dr. Brown felt we should talk to him. "She is twelve years old," I told him, "and if we get three more years with her we'd be very happy." He agreed, but still felt we should see Dr. Erickson before making our final decision. After telling him I would, Skeeter and I went home with our heads down. Once home, I released Skeeter from the carrier and she headed for parts unknown to lick her wound and sulk. I, on the other hand, headed for the kitchen and ate every sugar product I could find. We each have our ways of dealing with bad news.

After many more days of soul searching I had definitely decided to not do anything. I would check Skeeter for additional lumps and take action as needed. Hopefully, we will have many more years with her. If not, then I will have to live with the guilt. I can't put her through that surgery and chemo. When I told the doctor what I'd decided he said the cancer could attach itself to the liver and she might not develop more lumps. Great!

For now Skeeter is a happy, loving cat who runs through the house chasing imaginary items, gives tons of kisses and acts like a kitten again. I'll take this new attitude and live knowing that life is a crapshoot and we all could be dead in an instant. Skeeter could outlive me. We'll take it one day at a time.

Chapter 10

Rainy Days and Sundays

On a rainy Sunday morning I woke up around 5:30 to the sound of thunder and lightening. Should I drag myself out of that warm, cozy bed and go down and shut off the computer? Yes, we have the power strippy thing that's supposed to stop lightening, but I never trusted those things. Reluctantly, I crawled my way downstairs and closed all the programs I had open and then turned my attention to the hole in the ceiling of my office.

After adjusting the bucket I kept there for just such emergencies, I decided I should put a trash bag under it just in case the monsoons came and the leak became a torrent.

The ceiling had been dripping for about a year, starting out as a small maybe-it's- going-to-drip spot, and escalating into a full-blown river pouring into my office, ruining my parquet floors. When I first pointed it out to Max it was just a spot buckled in that wonder product, the blown ceiling. You know the stuff; it sheds all over the floor if you dare to touch it. And don't even think about patching. There is no humanly possible way to match a blown ceiling; the whole thing has to be repainted.

Of course, Max had ignored me. He had this crazy idea that if he ignored it, it would go away. It didn't. As the months passed each rain brought more threat that something bigger was to come. First there were the ceiling particles on the floor. Max still refused to look. Next was the first actual water spot. No response. Then the spot was bigger with two other places showing rain stain. I nagged, I pleaded, I tried every wifely urging I could. Finally, the monsoon came and the ceiling poured forth like a cloud opening to feed the grass after a long, parched summer. My office became the "River of Denial." Out came the buckets.

Max finally admitted there was a problem, went up on the roof and repaired it. After cutting a huge hole in my ceiling, patching and repairing it with a new piece of sheet rock, we waited for the next cloudburst. Everything went well for a while; the summer of 2003 was a dry one but when the rains came it was like the heavens were taking some kind of revenge on us. The storm pounded our house, battered my poor trees and poured rain in my office like it thought I needed a cleansing bath.

Now, fully awake, I decided to empty the dishwasher so I wouldn't have to later. Of course some of the maggots wanted their breakfast. I really hated to feed them at 6:00 a.m., knowing full well they'd expect a repeat at 8:00 when we eat. Being the sucker I am, I gave in and went around gathering up the rest of the troops to make sure they were really hungry. I noticed Rosey wasn't among them, and since she's usually the first one in line, I filled their plates and went looking for her. This was definitely not Rosey's style. I called, got down on my knees looking under furniture, but she was nowhere to be found. Max woke up from the light in his eyes and decided to join the search. Max and Rosey have a strange relationship; he pretends she doesn't exist and she doesn't know he even lives in the house.

We looked under the bed again, behind the sofa, under the sofa and checked every closet three times. No Rosey. After an hour had passed, I decided she must have gotten out. Of course, she would never go near the door no matter how many times I encouraged her to run away, but I knew she had to have gotten out when Max came home around midnight. After pulling on socks, shoes, pants, sweat-

shirt, rain scarf and a raincoat, I grabbed the flashlight and went cat hunting.

I called, I pleaded. I looked under the porch where the woodchuck lives shining the light in his face. He was not happy to see me. Why on earth do I keep him in a daily supply of sunflower seeds? Across the street, I peeked in a neighbor's garage that had been left open, hoping she'd taken refuge there. I saw my neighbor sitting in her living room. Oops! I don't want her calling the police thinking I'm a peeking Jane, so I scurried back to my side of the street.

Finally I admitted there was no way Rosey would ever leave a place where she gets three squares a day and can cause all the aggravation she wants. She had to be holed up somewhere in the house, either dead or dying. If my guys don't show up for food they are sick or dead. I've said it before, and it's worth repeating, my cats are P-I-G-S, hogs!

As I was planning Rosey's funeral, Max went back to bed and I wandered the house like a lost soul. Although Rosey never liked me I've always felt a kinship with her, an understanding. I stay out of her way and everyone lives happily ever after.

While I was wallowing in pity my mind raced to a doctor's appointment my mother had on Friday. Battling kidney problems, enduring dialysis three times a week, the nurse bonded with her. When I excused myself to go to the bathroom they started exchanging cat stories and by the time I returned Lori, the nurse, knew my whole cat history, and the two of them were plotting to get me to take in another cat. Lori had rescued a stray that had kittens and was trying to find homes for them. I said, "No way!"

As I sat there waiting to see if by some miracle Rosey would rise from the grave I already had her buried in, this exchange popped into my head: Was this God's way of saying I should take in this new cat?

Just as I was calling the mortuary ready to order her headstone, Rosey mysteriously appeared, walking out of my office. I'd looked there again and again. Nowhere to hide in there; two chairs, a desk, a bookcase, a curio cabinet, no place she could dig into and sleep. But who cared where she'd been, she has risen from the dead! Rosey is alive! I was overjoyed. Tears streamed down my face for the cat that never let herself love. Saying her name over and over, I ran and got her food, letting her know how much we'd missed her and how frightened we were when we couldn't find her. She ran from me. She doesn't mean it; she really loves me. I know it.

She took a spot on the steps in the living room and waited while I set her food dish down, then she hissed. As I looked lovingly into her eyes she gave me her usual I-hate-your-guts, is-this-what-you're-serving-for-breakfast look, and things were back to normal.

Chapter 11

Salem Takes a Poop

On May 25, 2004 I took Salem to the vet. His bowels were still bothering him and I'd tried everything I knew, but nothing worked. I'd even resorted to giving him enemas — not a pleasant task, but he was very willing to let me do anything to relieve his distress. The vet took a look at him, determined he would have to put him under and basically dig it out. Salem looked dehydrated so he also wanted to run some tests. I kissed Salem goodbye and told him I'd see him tomorrow.

The vet called at 8:30 in the morning to break the news that the tests were back and it didn't look good. From the test results, he said Salem's kidneys were not working, and although he didn't out and out say it, I got the impression we should put Salem to sleep. Max and I wanted to be there.

For the longest time Max and I held each other; I think Max was hurting more than I was. Although Max strongly resisted when I first brought Salem in, they became buddies, with Salem sitting in his lap every night while he attempted to read the paper. Max loved calling him "Bad Boy" in contrast to my "Sweet Salem." We were both crushed. As I dressed, recollections flashed through my head; the first time I saw Salem, the way he slept between Max and me at night, how he wouldn't allow me to kiss him on the mouth, no matter how much

I forced the issue. "Yuck", he said, "girl germs."

When I noticed a week ago that he wasn't going to the bathroom, I also noticed he wasn't finishing all his dinner. At times he wouldn't eat at all. He and the rest of the troops ate the good stuff, Science Diet® for cats, the light one to keep their girlish figures. Then I decided he needed to put on weight. Normally Salem was big and cuddly but now he was skin and bone, having lost almost three pounds. I ran out and got him Fancy Feast®. He scarfed down almost the whole can, so I determined he couldn't be that sick if he was eating.

At 10:00 a.m. Max and I entered the veterinarian's office with heavy hearts. We were told to have a seat as the vet was with someone. I asked if we could go in and see Salem while we were waiting, and after much debate we were given permission.

Salem looked so lost and afraid in the back of the cage. He didn't recognize me at first, and then he started crying. I picked him up and held him tight as the tears came. Max looked sick. The vet came into the room and told us we could go into one of the examination rooms. Salem had twisted himself into the sweater I was wearing and proceeded to twist so much that he was sitting behind me on the chair, completely wrapped up in my sweater.

The vet took forever to get to us. Our 10:00 a.m. appointment became 10:30 and finally at 10:35 it was time. After reviewing the test results with us, he gave us three options. First, was having an ultrasound to assess the condition of the kidneys (hope! there is hope!) to determine how we should proceed. Max said let's do it. This vet's office didn't do ultrasounds but he called Mission Med Vet, not far from his office, and they said to come right over.

While Salem was scrunched behind me on the chair I noticed how warm he was. I thought he had a fever, but when I stood up I found out the source of the heat. He had peed all over himself, my sweater, the chair and me. Picking him up, I held him tight. Was it fright he couldn't control his bladder, or he just had to go and was mad as hell at me? I don't really know.

Were we doing the right thing? Should we end his suffering right now and let him go on to a better place? I just didn't know but didn't want to forever wonder if maybe there was something we could have done and didn't.

Max headed for the other vet's office. Once there, the doctor came out and said it would be twenty to twenty-five minutes. She wouldn't let me go with Salem even though I wanted to. They had to shave his belly and she insisted it wouldn't hurt.

It seemed an eternity before the vet came out, but it was actually only forty-five minutes. She was very apologetic but it was so worth the wait. One kidney was perfectly healthy and the other one, though it had an infection and was smaller, meant Salem was nowhere near ready to be put to sleep. I wanted to kiss her. The infection would have to be addressed and at some point he would have to have his colon operated on. Her office had already called our vet and we headed back there so they could fill him full of fluids and get him started on antibiotics.

The vet didn't know how soon they could put him under anesthetic so they could remove the poop so we said goodbye and left him there once more. This time a weight had been lifted from my heart.

At 6:32 p.m. Dr Goodman called and said they had inserted a catheter, were pumping Salem full of fluids and giving him antibiotics. It was a wait and see pattern, with Dr. Erickson taking Salem home to keep an eye on him. Tomorrow they were going to recheck his creatine and maybe then they could put him under anesthesia to dig out that poop.

On Thursday I spoke with Dr. Erickson twice; the first time he let me know they were going to run more tests and would call me with the results. True to his word, Dr. Erickson called and told me Salem's BUN and creatine — whatever those are — were better. For now, he was going to give Salem an enema and maybe later put him under to, remove the blockage. My God, how that must hurt to have all that shit backed up. Salem must be in terrible pain.

Friday morning I called and spoke to the receptionist who relayed the progress from the doctor. They got some of the poop out but it didn't sound as if they'd operated. She didn't know if they had but would ask the doctor. It really didn't matter as long as something was coming out. They were going to try to get more out today. I wanted to know when Salem could come home. She didn't know. Then I asked about the bill. As much as I didn't want to know I thought I had better prepare them for the fact that we didn't have any money. As of two days before, the bill was $460; I just about shit because it cost me a fortune to get my cat to shit.

The ultrasound was another $239; we were sinking deeper in debt, with no end in sight. I told the receptionist we were going to have to work out a payment plan. They required half down and the rest in payments. Salem had already been there three days, if they kept him another three the bill could double. When I relayed this to Max he looked at me and turned green. Ah, the joys of parenthood.

Since I hadn't seen Salem in two days, I was afraid he'd think I had deserted him. I'm never sure what the right thing to do is. Should I visit a sick animal, or not? My fear is if they see me, will they think I am taking them home and they'll be more upset when I can't? I didn't want him to think I didn't love him, so I thought maybe I'd stop by.

Saturday morning Dr. Erickson said he was able to get some more stool out and they were trying not to put him under anesthetic. Yesterday they got quite a bit and plan on more today. He drew blood this morning and was waiting on the results to get back before he could say whether Salem could go home today or have to stay over the weekend. With it being Memorial Day weekend I wouldn't be able to get him until Tuesday. I asked the vet about whether I should see Salem or not. Sometimes it helps the animal and other times it doesn't, he said; the problem is figuring out which it will be. What the hell, I would go ahead and stop by anyway and take the chance.

As I looked through the bars at this helpless creature I felt ashamed I hadn't come by every day. Salem looked like he had lost his best

friend and was all alone in the world. At first he didn't recognize me. I called his name softly, without a response, but as I put my fingers through the cage something registered when he saw my nails. He recognized my peach polish. Yea! Mommy's here. He rushed over and rubbed himself against the bars. Back and forth he went, tangling the IV so much I was afraid he would pull it out. I tried to calm him down, but he didn't care. He was so excited that I didn't know whether to open the door or not, and finally gave in to my motherly urges and threw open the door to love all over him. He was so happy to see me.

I stayed about thirty minutes, then spoke to the doctor, who thought I might get to take Salem home that day. It was already noon and they closed at 2:00 on Saturdays. The vet said he would let me know, so I gave my cell phone number to the receptionist. At 4:30 I finally heard from the vet. I could pick Salem up Sunday at 6:00, when he would be back in the office. I was ecstatic and said I would see him Sunday.

I've always wondered if my pets are being taken care of properly. Not knowing if the people I am relying on are good people or have a lot of issues is so scary. When I found Dr. Erickson was taking Salem home at night I knew I had found someone I could trust with my life.

Sunday, true to his word, Dr. Erickson was at the office. He was able to get all the poop out of Salem and gave me a 21-day supply of pills for him. Salem had to go back on Tuesday so they could draw blood and continue to monitor his BUN and creatine. Although Salem is doing better, he is definitely not out of the woods by any means and the long-term prognosis doesn't sound that great. The more the vet talked, the more I wondered if we shouldn't have put him down. But for now, I didn't care; I had my Salem Bah-bee and I was taking him home to shower him with love and kisses till he begged for mercy.

Salem cried in the car on the way home and I kept telling him he'd be okay. Once we reached the driveway, I set his cage on the ground and he saw friendly territory. At the front door he was yelling to get out of the carrier. Once in the house he ran around like a kitten. All the other cats came up and smelled him but they quickly lost interest and went back to their business.

Salem ate four times that night. He hadn't eaten much at the vet's, but now that he was home his appetite kicked in. Unfortunately, he was on a special diet and by the next day the newness had worn off and he decided to be finicky. No matter how much I coaxed he wouldn't eat the recommended diet and kept trying to get to what the others were eating. Of course, they all wanted what he was eating. All day he lay around. We loved on him, but as the day wore on he drooped more and more.

Tuesday morning I called the vet and they told me to bring him in at 1:30. He ate a little breakfast but not enough to get his strength back to where it needed to be.

Salem was not prepared to go back to that horrible place and fought me tooth and nail. The vet looked him over, took more blood and gave me more food to try. Pleading poverty, I paid a portion of the bill and got Salem back in the car. Dr. Goodman was going to call later with the test results that would hopefully prove this was just an infection and not kidney failure.

About an hour and a half after we arrived home Dr. Goodman called. He had good news. Everything looked good and Salem could eat anything he wanted. Salem has been healed.

"Oops, we made a mistake," he called and said 10 minutes later. The tech had used dog serum, or some such crap, that altered the tests. Salem was not out of the woods. Although the results were much better than yesterday, we were still in that wait and see holding pattern. Needless to say, I was not a happy camper and had to resist the urge to tell him what an ass he and his tech were.

By Friday Salem was back to his old, new self. Strange what facing death can do to a person, and in this case a cat. That morning he got down off the bed and went over to Domino to wrestle with him. Remembering how mean Salem normally was, Domino told him to

forget it. Salem seemed to have this aura about him now, peaceful and in tune with the universe; respectful to his peers, he no longer attacked but promoted harmony wherever he flopped down. Waiting for the bomb to drop, I thought surely when he was fully recovered the old Salem would emerge; the, "get out of my way, who told you, you could lie in my sunspot," type of guy that he was. For the time being we enjoyed the loving, new and improved version.

Still having problems pooping, I gave Salem enemas every other day. Dr. Goodman let me know he had called in two prescriptions that Salem was to take for his colon; one was a laxative. The company I had to get it from was out of town so I had to use my credit card for the $77.10 medicine. Fortunately they were liquids, which was a lot easier to get down Salem than a pill was. In the beginning Salem was so weak he didn't care what I gave him, but by the second week of pills the vet had given him he was spitting them out. One day I found two of his pills under my bed. Not knowing if they were from that day or from another, I gave them to him again.

Over the next three weeks I gave Salem his medicine and every day he showed signs of improvement. I even saw him poop twice and Max thinks he saw him go once. By the time his pills ran out he was his old self again, wrestling with Little One and terrorizing Priss. When the medicine ran out I made an appointment at the vet's to bring Salem in for tests.

Dr. Erickson looked Salem over, took blood and said everything looked good, so far. Salem's fur was starting to shine, he had lots of energy and I shared with the doctor about bowel movements. The doctor was glad to hear everything was coming out OK. He confirmed Salem would have to take the medicine for the rest of his life and he would call later that day with the test results.

When the results came back Dr. Erickson didn't sound as hopeful as he had earlier. Although they were better, Salem wasn't doing as well as expected and the vet wanted Salem to do another round of pills for an additional three weeks. Not sure what the long-term prognosis was, I didn't ask. I'd rather just take it one day at a time. Three weeks later Max and I took Salem back to the vet. He had been doing great; eating regular, taking his medicine and as loving as can be. At the last check-up Salem's weight was back up to 10.5 pounds and was now 11. He had only gained half a pound, but as Max said, at least he's gaining and not losing. The doctor took blood and we waited for the results.

Salem was so cute the entire time. He hated going to the vet and it took both Max and me to get him in his carrier. I took a towel with me so he could wrap himself up in it, which he did the minute he came out of the cage. He was so afraid he cried the entire way there and back. I held him at the doctor's and he kept grabbing my hand. I had to touch him and love him. He was shaking. I kept telling him he would be okay but he was too scared to listen. On the way home I let him look out the window to see he was going home, but he didn't settle down till we pulled into the driveway.

Dr. Erickson called at 7:30 that night to tell us Salem's test results were worse than last time. He explained chronic kidney failure and the lasting effects. He said his BUN and creatine were elevated. This was not good. Although he said he could bounce back occasionally, he also said the Feline Immunodeficiency Virus may be causing problems. I was to watch him very closely and keep him on the new antibiotic. If he gets worse; vomiting, diarrhea or not eating I was to bring him right in.

There is another pill we could give him but he wanted to hold off on it to see how Salem did, and recommended getting another sonogram. Salem was to go back in 10-14 days to recheck the BUN and creatine.

This was not the news I was expecting; Salem had been doing great lately and didn't appear sick at all. The doctor was also surprised at the results and felt Salem looked great too but couldn't find an explanation.

Over the next year Salem limped along. On the outside he looked healthy, but his kidneys kept failing and his bowel problems got worse until not even an enema worked. In the end it was fruitless to continue. On March 5, 2005 at 1:00 p.m. Salem drew his last breath. Goodbye, Bad Boy. We will always miss you. You will be forever in our hearts. Thank you for coming to our house to live.

Chapter 12

Not Again

On June 24, 2004, another lump appeared. It was the size of a marble. Skeeter seemed unfazed but I was beside myself. What had I done? I rolled the dice and lost. How could I do this to my precious Skeeter, my healing cat?

For the next three months I monitored Skeeter. Knowing I needed to act swiftly, I had to put Skeeter's health on the backburner. My mother was diagnosed with colon cancer at the same time Skeeter's lump appeared. Mother had been diagnosed with kidney failure a year and a half before and I was taking her to dialysis three times a week. The doctors kept ignoring her when she complained for months of a sharp pain in her stomach. No one knew why she also had constant diarrhea for years, either. Being 89 and stubborn, she had resisted seeing a doctor until she started dialysis, and by then the tumor had grown to the size of a grapefruit.

After spending weeks at the hospital with her, she was moved to a rehab hospital where I continued camping out. Once I felt Mother was out of danger and I could trust the people who were caring for her, I scheduled an appointment for Skeeter. Dr. Erickson operated and she came through just fine. Because of the weight she had gained in the year since the last lump, he had to remove a fair amount of fat. Cancer has roots and he was afraid it had spread into her tummy; he

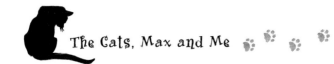

performed his first cat liposuction on Skeeter.

By January 2005 Skeeter's health was getting worse. She had been acting lethargic, her breathing was labored and I had a feeling it was something more than a tummy ache. Mid-December of 2004 my mother had come to live with us and couldn't be left alone, so Max volunteered to take Skeet to the vet. Well, not exactly volunteered, I volunteered him. The vet ran some of his famous "tests" and called me with the results. From all indications, he guessed she had pancreatitis. Using the usual array of words I didn't understand, he said he wanted Skeeter to have an ultrasound. Of course he couldn't do it at his place; I needed to take her to the Emergency MedVet.

I called first thing the next morning and they got her right in. Again, poor Max got Skeet duty. This doctor noticed her difficulty in breathing and took an x-ray. There wasn't any need to do an ultrasound; Skeeter's lungs were covered in cancerous nodes and the doctor recommended we put her down. He said she would suffer terribly if we brought her home, and would die anyway within two weeks. He suggested putting her to sleep was the humane thing to do. I threw on some clothes and asked Max to go with me. I hated to leave my mother by herself, but I couldn't face this alone; I just couldn't.

I had reservations about letting Emergency MedVet put Skeet down due to a prior experience with one of my mother's cats. Archie was very ill and it was decided to put him to sleep. I said fine, but requested they let me be there for his final moments on earth. The attending vet said I could. I was then told to wait in the reception area and she would come get me when they were ready. After twenty minutes passed I complained to the receptionist that the vet hadn't come for me. I was ignored. When the vet finally came out of the death chamber, I immediately confronted her. She became hateful and full of herself. "Why, we never let anyone back there. No one can be with their animal when they are put to sleep," she insisted. I resisted the urge to tell her what a bitch she was. I knew that arguing was futile, but I needed to vent, so I challenged and repeated what she had told me. My voice raised a few decibels as I let her know she had told me I could sit with Archie until he was gone. It didn't do any good; she was right and I was wrong.

I made up my mind I wasn't going to let that happen to Skeeter, so I immediately confronted the receptionist. "Dr. Harnett said I could be with my cat when he put her down. The last time I was here I was told this and they had lied." On and on I ranted. The receptionist, poor girl, told me exactly what the doctor had said, they always let people be with their animals when they are put to sleep. She tried her best to be kind and showed Max and me to a room where we were to wait and they would bring Skeeter in.

After only ten minutes I got tired of waiting and went out to the front. I finally found the receptionist and told her to bring me my cat; this was time I could be spending with her. They brought the cat.

Skeeter was glad to see us. I held her as she squirmed, but I managed to kiss and hug her pretty good. She kept trying to get away. It was strange because she wanted to go to Max. She had always been my cat, but now, in death, she wanted a big, strong man to hold her. It hurt but I let him have her and after awhile she settled in between the two of us. We got to spend about twenty minutes of bonding time with her before the doctor came in. He explained the procedure and then put in an IV that would take away my beautiful, precious Skeeter. She fought at first, but as the poison took effect she became still. The doctor told us her eyes would probably stay open but he didn't say anything about her tongue being caught in her open mouth. Gently, he opened her mouth and pushed her tongue back in. I tried to close her eyes but could only get them shut halfway. They popped back open as fast as I shut them.

This doctor was very compassionate and told us how sorry he was. We would have her remains in about two weeks. He said we could stay with her awhile if we wanted; of course we did. As I stood there full of grief, crying my heart out, I suddenly realized there was another person in the room grieving with me. I looked up and Max was crying as hard as I was. I often forget how much these animals mean to him.

When we got home life just went on. I went about my business, but with a heavy heart and big hole in my gut. BeBe ran around the house confused. He smelled my jacket and looked at me. How could I tell him his mom will never come home? How would I tell him the nurturing mother that took care of him since the day he arrived would no longer be there for him? I held him; loved him; told him what happened, but I couldn't tell him why life is so cruel. I don't know if he understood me but I feel he did. I think he'd known for a long time that Skeeter would be going away and now his turn to be the healer had come.

For several months after Skeeter's last bout with cancer BeBe had been sleeping with me in Skeeter's spots. He slept against my back when it hurt and did the kneading thing. One morning I woke up with a crick in my neck and he positioned himself so he could put one paw at the base of my neck; he softly kneaded and applied just the lightest pressure. Within a few minutes my neck was fine and I was up and about. BeBe took over as the head of the pack when Charlie died and then as "healer of the mom" for Skeeter.

I had sixteen more months with Skeeter and I made good use of that time. I loved her, held her and told her how special she was and how much I appreciated all she had done for me. She had come to me when I needed her and it was time to let go. She lived a full life for those next twelve years and six months. She had a family that loved her and she is sorely missed. Farewell, faithful friend. Sleep well.

Chapter 13

Mr. No Namie

In the spring of 2004, a neighbor knocked on my door one evening with a cat at his feet and asked if it was mine. A look down revealed a small ball of black fur with huge golden eyes looking up at me with a lost look on his face! As I stood there holding open the screen door, the little guy walked in and made himself at home. I protested and said no way, not mine, but the little guy walked around and introduced himself to the rest of the troops. He said "Hey" to BeBe and "How's it going?" to Little One. Domino received a nod and the strange kitten smiled at Priss.

The neighbor said the little guy had been hanging around his house and another neighbor thought he might be one of my brood that had escaped. I assured him mine were all accounted for. When he asked if I would take the little fur ball, I told him I couldn't afford any more and I added that Max would kill me if I took in another one. Noticing how this cat was extremely attached to this neighbor, I pointed it out. He said he was a dog person.

After they left I started to worry what would happen to the little tyke. But then I wondered if death had sent him. Was he waiting for one of my guys to die? Every time one of the kids got sick there seemed to be another cat waiting in the wings to step in and take his place. Was this cat to be the new kid on the block?

I didn't see the cat very often. Periodically he would stop by and say hello, asking for a handout. As the months passed there were periods when I wouldn't see him for weeks and then, out of the blue, he would show up and stay for several days. Then just as suddenly as he appeared he would vanish.

Not wanting to get attached, but wanting to give the cat an identifying label, I called him No Name, which quickly became, due to his attitude, Mr. No Name, and then finally settling on the more prestigious handle of Mr. No Namie, pronounced "No Naaa mee."

In July he hung around for quite awhile and I tried to make friends with him. The longer he was on the streets the wilder he got. I had hoped our neighbor, Vic, would take him in, but that obviously didn't happen. Mr. No Namie didn't trust and didn't like to be touched. After about the third week of his stay, I was able to pet him on the back while he ate, but if I approached him he would run to another section of the deck. If I tried to pet him he would attack me, and I bear several scars from his attacks. I never gave up though.

He must have been getting fed somewhere else as he was filled out very nicely. Maybe Vic and some of the other neighbors fed him; he didn't have the haggard look of a stray. When he came to me in July he looked long and thin and didn't have a stomach on him, causing me to wonder if he was a she and that she had kittens somewhere. Call me crazy, but I was looking forward to that new kitten smell, the look of wonderment on a new face, the innocence of new life. But No Namie didn't bring any kittens, at least not to me. Feeling under his belly one night as he ate dinner I couldn't find any nipples protruding.

I wish I didn't worry so about things I can't control. That July was filled with storms and when Mr. No Namie didn't come home for breakfast I had visions of him and his kittens being washed away in a storm drain and drowning. When he didn't show up for dinner as well, I knew a car had hit him.

For all the worrying I did, I might as well have brought him inside, but the other cats didn't like him. At first he would attack them

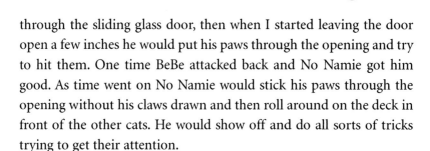

through the sliding glass door, then when I started leaving the door open a few inches he would put his paws through the opening and try to hit them. One time BeBe attacked back and No Namie got him good. As time went on No Namie would stick his paws through the opening without his claws drawn and then roll around on the deck in front of the other cats. He would show off and do all sorts of tricks trying to get their attention.

One morning after he'd finished his breakfast, I went outside to give him some treats; next to milk, he loved treats best. Slowly I bent down and held out my hand. He was beginning to trust me and I wanted to show him he had nothing to fear from me or mine. BeBe snuck out the door behind me as Mr. No Namie was eating. I didn't say anything, just slowly laid down the treats in front of No Namie and walked to the end of the deck. BeBe was sniffing everything he could as fast as he could knowing he was in deep trouble. I didn't say anything as I scooped BeBe up. I didn't hit or yell or scream, "You idiot, get in the house. This cat can tear you apart."

Once inside, I slid the door partway closed, open about three to four inches. No Namie came over and put his paw through, starting to hit at BeBe. As I bent down to tell him it was all right, he took a swipe at me and got my face. I closed the door. I thought I knew why he was so mad, and didn't blame him; he was the outdoor cat and BeBe was the indoor cat. The deck belonged to him and I wasn't to let them out on his domain. The deck and the yard were his.

I knew he was lonesome, as I'd seen it in several of the other cats before I took them in. Miss Priss, Salem and Huey often yearn for the free life, and interacting with Mr. No Namie must have had them thinking of their own days living on the streets, running through the tall grass at night in the field next to our house, sunbathing in the afternoons, going from place to place seeing wondrous things. How envious they were, but at the same time how comfortable they were living with me. When they would venture out they wouldn't stay long. They would explore, but only inside the fence, never trying to jump it.

never fully making a commitment to leave. Like Domino years before, maybe they too decided this was their home and this is where they would stay.

Mr. No Namie came often to eat, sometimes three times a day. I never refused him and always made sure he was well fed. One day, three days before Halloween, he was sunning himself on the deck railing and I checked on him often. One time when I looked out I saw a neighbor's dog on my deck with a slurpy "Which way did they go, George?" look on his face. He was a gentle dog who loved to roam the neighborhood, and wouldn't hurt a fly, but No Namie didn't know that and he was gone from his spot. I must have just missed him, so I shooed the dog away and went looking for No Namie. I called his name again and again, and when he didn't come I figured he ran under the porch and would be out in time for dinner. Evening came and went.

I kept beating myself up. I should have brought him in. All kinds of horrible thoughts were racing through my head over the next week. I just knew someone had caught him and was torturing him. I should never have left him out with so many crazy people out there. From my work at a non-profit that treated survivors of child abuse, I heard terrible stories about people torturing black cats at Halloween time. They gave me nightmares that I have to this day.

For weeks I looked for Mr. No Namie. I'd drive up and down the streets, walk across neighbors' yards calling, "Mr. No Namie, Mr. No Namie." People surely thought I'd lost my mind, but if I know my neighbors, they probably thought that of me a long time ago. Anyway, I didn't care. I was devastated. As much as I didn't want another cat, I didn't want anything to happen to him. I felt it was my duty to protect him from the evils that lurk in the shadows. I really missed him and have to admit I really wanted him but didn't want to say so. My home may be small, but he would have had plenty of love. The others would have accepted him; they always do.

Just when I finally accepted that Mr. No Namie was gone, he

appeared. Just like that. On the morning of February 18th, I opened the blinds and there he was waiting for breakfast. Only this time he was bigger and more filled out, like he had found a good home with loving people who fed him well. When I opened the slider and greeted him, he looked up at me as if to say, "Enough chit chat; where's the food?" Eagerly I obliged and filled a plate full of canned food and dry for him along with a big bowl of milk. As I set the food on the deck I reached over to pet him. We were back to square one; no petting, no movement, no anything. It was wham-bam-thank-you, ma'am. He ate his food and was on his way.

He may have been running away from home or just taking a day to visit his old haunts, but I didn't care. He was alive and well and that's all that mattered. I could sleep at night without worrying. I still look for him every morning, but so far he hasn't come back. When I began to doubt that I saw him, I asked Max if he had seen No Namie but he said no. Was he really here or was it his ghost come to tell me he was okay? Either way, he remembered me.

He knows he's loved and the door is always open and the food dish full. I'll continue my watch with a hopeful heart that he'll come back this way someday. But for now, "Good night, Mr. No Namie. Sleep well, wherever you are."

Chapter 14

Nine the Hard Way

March 29, 2005, my mother died, and six weeks later I moved her two cats, Pywacket and Murphy, in with me. It was a long two-year battle, but Mother finally said enough and quit dialysis; 29 days later she passed away.

Mom had Pywacket and Murphy seven to eight years; I'm not sure which. A friend gave Pywacket to her; Murphy showed up at her doorstep one "dark and stormy night." Before Mom's illness I'd never interacted with either one of them much. They only came out of their hiding spots when I offered food and as soon as their tummies were full they were gone, never to be seen, by me at least, until the next feeding. Once Mother went into the hospital Max and I took over their care and feeding, though with me having to be at the hospital day and night the duties fell mostly to Max. Murphy and Max bonded more, but Pywacket respected and periodically actually rubbed up against him.

Py was a skittish cat and afraid more than mean. Mom had a good relationship with her so I knew she wasn't a shithead like Rose. Although Py wanted love she needed to know she could trust before giving it.

As Mother's illness progressed and it was obvious she would never be coming back to her home of 40 years, I started the dreadful task of packing up her beloved memories. In the beginning I'd spend only an hour or two between hospital runs. I'd fill a box or two and then sit down with Murphy and comfort him. I'd lie and tell him his mommy was coming home and everything would be all right. I'm not sure if the lies were for him or me. Once in a while Py would come over and let me pet her.

It's hard rummaging through another person's things, almost an invasion of privacy. Not that Mom had anything to hide, damn it. That would have been fun, finding something really interesting about my mother, but Mom was an open book. She told her troubles to friends and strangers alike, almost to the point of embarrassment. Unfortunately, I think I have inherited that trait. I HATE it when I tell people too much about myself and always walk away going, "Why did I tell that person that? Am I nuts?" No, I'm just being my mom, overly friendly and thinking everyone cares.

Mom was a good, kind person who got a raw deal in life. Deserted by an abusive husband she found herself living in a strange town with three small children and no friends. She persevered though, sometimes working three jobs. As poor as we were, she taught us the finer points of life. She taught me and my brothers to walk into a place like we owned it, holding our heads up high, not letting people know the soles of our shoes had holes and our underwear was ragged and torn. If we had been raised in another household there are so many things she introduced us to that we may never have seen.

Mother had a trained operatic voice and sang with the Kansas City Philharmonic for many years, so my older brother Ronnie and I got to participate whenever they needed children. I loved the costumes and especially the ballet dancers. I think my brother liked that we didn't have to go to school the next day after the late night rehearsals. Mom said it was more important for us to be in an opera; we could always catch up on schoolwork. How many kids can say they got to be on stage in a production of *Tosca*?

As broke as we were, Mother always found the dollar a week so I could take ballet lessons when I was twelve and an extra quarter for me to have a hot dog and root beer at Woolworth's dime store next door to the dance studio. I've never had a root beer or hotdog that can match that meal. Unable to sew, Mother had to pay someone to make my costumes for the recitals I participated in several times a year. Knowing what a great sacrifice this was to the family, by the time I was thirteen I told her I didn't want to dance anymore; that I had lost interest. I wish she hadn't believed me, since my one dream in 1958 was to defect to Russia so I could dance with the prestigious ballet troupes there. I felt the American ballet companies were far inferior to the Russian.

When I was fourteen Mom found the money for me to take piano lessons. This didn't last long though, as it was hard practicing the piano without actually having the instrument in front of me. Pretending I was sitting at a keyboard, I would play on the kitchen table, my knees, anything I could trying to hear the notes. After only a year, when it became obvious Mom could not swing the money for a Baby Grand, I quit. I wasn't very good anyway. My little brother, Brian, must have gotten all my musical talent; he grew up to become the internationally renowned, contemporary jazz keyboardist Max Groove.

Seeing my mother in such a fragile state was hard; she had always been the backbone of the family. Through the years, as she got older and the years caught up to her, what bothered her most was her mind wasn't as strong as it once had been. Years before she had been tested and her IQ was 143; she was definitely Mensa material. When I pointed out she had already said something, she hated it and asked me not to tell her because it was too upsetting. It was so hard listening to her repeat herself over and over but I would grit my teeth and silently scream inside. Now I wish I could hear her stories one more time. I wouldn't care how many times I'd heard them before.

Mother had a vast collection of interesting things, like an old copy of *Gone with the Wind* — second edition, not first. I checked; damn!

The Cats, Max and Me

As I was laying claim to her possessions there were two items I didn't have a clue what to do with; Pywacket and Murphy. Mother was frantic about their plight. I told her maybe, possibly, I could take Murphy (I didn't have the guts to tell this to Max), but there was no way I would take Pywacket; Py pissed under Mom's bed. The smell in her bedroom was so intolerable I don't know how she slept there. It must be true what they say; as we get older our senses go. Her taste buds had gone, as well as her sense of smell. Lucky her.

Max had cleaned out under her bed once. He cut the carpet away and used cleaning products that guaranteed to clean up piss. I increased the number of litter boxes in the house and encouraged Py to use them, but she still liked under Mother's bed the most. Mom had told us Py and Murphy didn't get along and that Murphy terrorized Py, but once they were the only ones in the house they formed a bond that strengthened with each month that passed. Both Max and I noticed it and by the time the house was ready to be put up for sale they were inseparable.

Not able to take on one more life to feed, clothe and bathe, I looked through the Yellow Pages for a place to board Py and Murphy and found a place called Pete and Mac's. First, I was going to board them at my vets, but thought they needed more than lying in a cage all day listening to dogs bark. Pete and Mac's Recreational Resort for Pets was preferred by area veterinarians and offered dog and cat lodging, a retail boutique and bakery, plus professional grooming. They were the latest in doggie day care, and also groomed animals on the premises, plus, they were close to where I lived. So I checked them out.

I had seen this place on one of the morning news shows but nothing could have prepared me for the extreme lengths people will go to so that their pets are happy. The boutique and bakery are in the lobby and I could see through a large window into the doggie day room. The dogs were well behaved and appeared very happy. Several came to the window and said hello. They all had big smiles on their faces and many ran around and around in the room. Some were sleeping on lit-

tle beds that were equipped with little mattresses. I could only specu-
late that they were exhausted from playing doggie games.

I was given the full tour, which included a peek into the room
where the dogs sleep. What I saw was truly amazing. Each cubicle had
glass blocks for walls so the dogs didn't feel claustrophobic. Many had
those cute metal beds with mattresses and several had murals painted
on the walls. Some even had televisions so the dogs could watch
Animal Planet, I was told. After seeing that the dogs were well cared
for I toured the cat room. Py and Murphy would never want to leave
this place. One full wall was a large window with bird feeders hanging
outside. The cages were arranged so they could watch nature 24/7. A
handler would come in several times a day to play with the cats and
take them out of their cages so they can exercise. I met a cat by the
name of Lady that had been deserted by its owner and Pete and Mac's
kept her. These were my kind of people. I signed Py and Murphy up.

In order to be accepted at the resort of pets I needed to update
their shots. Although Mother had always been very good about seeing
her pets were well taken care her of, her health took precedence the
past year or two. I made an appointment with my vet and for only
$237 Py and Murphy were both ready for school. Well, not exactly.
With all the shit going on in my life Py and Murphy hadn't gotten the
care they were used to, like regular brushing. Py's chest was badly
knotted and Murphy's whole body needed shaving. He was able to
keep the head, legs and tail hair but his entire body hair had to go. He
looked adorable but he didn't think so and was traumatized beyond
repair. By the time I checked them into the boarding school they were
a nervous wreck. I had them put in connecting cages to make them
feel better.

Whenever I could, I visited and brought them treats that I shared
with whomever was being boarded at the time. I made friends with
Lady and would love to have taken her home. Py and Murphy didn't
take to being boarded as well as the others. When I would take one out
they would claw their way back in. The longer they were there the

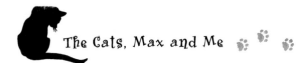
more scared they were. Everyone was lovely, but Py and Murphy were convinced they were going to be sold into slavery or served up for someone's Sunday supper.

While Py and Murphy were tearing up boarding school their owner was wreaking havoc at my place. When Mother first came to live with us I gave up the room I used as my home office. I loved that room and resented having anyone else in it; but it was the best room for Mom as it had a full bathroom attached. It was hard getting used to people being in my house every day, but I don't know how I would have managed without Hospice and Assisted Health. These people are very well trained, with a capital T. Mom was cleansed, clothed, and fed before I could even get dressed each day. Someone cleaned my house twice a week and my bathrooms had never shone so much since the day I moved in.

For the three months Mom was at my home I alternated between loving and hating her. I functioned on one to two hours sleep a night and was relieved when she decided to go off the dialysis; guilty but relieved; devastated, but glad it was going to be over soon. I was going to lose my mommy. What would life be like without a mother to blame for my troubles and offer support when I screwed up?

Mothers and daughters are a complex pair. Our relationship grew strained through years, but I loved her very much. I'm not sure she knew that at the end, but I tried to show her and told her often. There's a big gap in my life without my mother and maybe I can show her how much I loved her by taking in the two most important creatures that were in her life when she died. Welcome home, Pywacket and Murphy!

Chapter 15

The Smurf

Although this book has been about my relationships with cats, I can't forget a special dog that was in my life. Muffy lived with us for almost fifteen years before she passed away. She was an extraordinary sweetie who would have taken a bullet for me. So, please allow me this one indulgence, to share this magnificent animal with you.

Muffy "The Wonder Dog" was a Chow-Chow, a fearless guard dog, always alert, always ready to attack. As long as it wasn't anything more harmful than a leaf, that is. Muffy barked at every sound and was scared of her shadow. When danger presented itself she would insist I investigate first. There were many midnight hours I'd coax and coax trying to get her to go down the stairs to see what peril lurked. But there was no way she was going to confront an intruder. No siree!

Max is a musician and away from the house most evenings so I paid $400 for guard duty training when Muffy was young, to make me feel safe. But all it did was make Muffy a big 'fraidy cat. She hated the instructor, and with good cause I discovered. He was a psycho nut who wanted to make her into a killing machine. After one month of kill, crush, destroy, Muffy became scared to death of men; except for Max that is. She loved him and showed it by shaking herself on his black slacks whenever the opportunity arose. Afraid of heights, loud sounds, and pitch-black rooms, Muffy also hated air conditioning.

She was stingy with her love and would laugh her head off when I'd try to make her kiss me. Sometimes she'd give in, and with just the littlest flick of her black tongue, she'd gently brush over my hand ever so lightly. This amused her to no end. The more I'd beg for kisses, the more she'd refuse; I could tell it was a big joke to her.

She was the first animal Max and I had together. I was looking for a West Highland Terrier and instead wound up with this small ball of beige fur with big sad eyes. She was such a sweet little thing I had to take her home. She was a joy in my life, and when I was sick she was a great comfort to me because I knew down deep, if need be, she would be there for me.

There was a time Muffy's heroics were put to the test. I was lying in bed reading a magazine and as I turned the page I saw what I thought was a red piece of thread sticking out of the top. Curious as to what it was, I flipped to the next page and a big ugly, red spider fell on me. Of course I screamed, and before the next sound came out of my mouth, Muffy was at the side of my bed ready to do bodily harm to whatever had caused her mistress distress. Her ears were standing up, her body taut, with muscles flexed. She jumped a few inches off the ground and ran back and forth the length of my bed. She was a killing machine. The training had paid off! I knew then that no real harm would ever come to me if Muffy was around. She was a remarkable dog.

Poor Muffy didn't care for the cats much but she tolerated them as best she could, unless one of them licked her chew bone. Then she'd growl until the offender backed away. Every year for Christmas she got a new chew bone among her presents, and she was great about putting on a Santa hat and having her yearly picture taken. But boy, there'd better be a new chew bone in that pile of gifts. There always was.

When Muffy was one year old we threw her a birthday party, complete with Blue Smurf birthday cake, hats and plates after the cartoon characters. Max had nicknamed Muffy after them. I invited everyone I could think of, including the neighbors; what was so remarkable is that ten people showed up, on time and with presents. Some even brought their pets.

Muffy knew she was special that day. She examined every present, most of the Smurf paraphernalia, and even wore a hat without a fuss. She had birthday cake and, amazingly, attempted to blow out the candles.

We had fun with Muffy and I was always thinking up some crazy scenario to put her in. For her first Halloween I bought her a Batman costume and Max and I drove her all over town trick or treatin'; first to my mom's and then to Max's sister, Phyllis. Again, everyone treated her like this was the most natural thing to do. They all had dog biscuits ready for her sack. The corners of her mouth were turned way up that night. She liked being the center of attention.

My girlfriend Billie used to own a pet store and would groom Muffy for me. I'd insist she put bows in her fur and paint her toenails and she'd come out looking as pretty as a French Poodle. In 1983, when we got her, bows tied at the neck were the fashion rage and I bought Muffy an assortment of her own. She wore her green and brown plaid preppy bow a lot, but her favorite was a red and white checked cloth napkin I'd tie around her neck when we ordered pizza. Her job was to wait at the front door and tell us when the "Pizza Dude" had arrived. Her pay was a slice of Pizza Hut® Supreme; she was in doggy heaven.

Muffy was a great dog. She'd chase the birds out of the yard when they pecked her on top of the head, and fell asleep while balanced on the top step of the stairs. She was quite a sight; the step was too small for her body so she'd lie on her right side with her feet hanging over, falling fast asleep in the afternoon sun.

She never moved much; we usually had to step over her. Her favorite spot was the farthest from the door in the bedroom, next to the closet. When Max came home at night he'd trip over her as he tried to feel his way into bed. She'd grumble at him and fall back asleep.

When I was afraid at night and all alone, it was good to know there was someone to watch over me. Thank you, Muffy. You are loved and missed and will never be forgotten.

Epilogue

Life in Balance

Max bought me a T-shirt that says, "Every Life Should Have Nine Cats." I couldn't agree more. Robyn Green, one of my alternative healers, pointed this out to me early on. She said nine is my lucky number. I know that now and just have to accept the fact that there will always be nine cats around me to love and take care of. I've toyed with the idea of moving to a farm so I can have 100. Although I would be in heaven I'm not so sure about Max. He supports my fetish but I think he does have his limits. I always say I'm going to be one of those old ladies they find dead, with hundreds of cats in her house, eating their deceased, beloved mistress.

My love for animals, especially cats, is ingrained in me and I don't think I could survive without cats. I love the very essence of their being. I could not imagine my life without them. They have brought such peace and joy to my life that it would be fruitless to ignore their existence. My life has taken several twists and turns, and through it all my babies have been there with me. Domino still sucks my armpit and is now the main man in my life (sorry Max). He loves to wake me up in the middle of the night by sitting on my chest, licking my mouth and crying till I wake up and put him in his position to nurse. One leg has developed a spur and he limps a little, but hopefully he will be with me for many years to come. Miss Priss is still alive and kicking with maybe a small sign that she may have AIDS; her nose has an ulcer on it that the vet had to cauterize with silver nitrate. He prescribed an antibiotic and said some cats live for years with no signs so we're hoping for the best.

BeBe is crazy as always, and Little One loves his mama more and more each day. He has to sit in my lap, lie next to me and be under my feet constantly. Huey is as fat as ever and loving it. Rosey still has that love/hate thing going on. Max still would like to get rid of her, but I keep holding out hope that one day she'll surprise me and walk right up and give me a great big kiss. I can see it now. Rosey and her fabulous mom taking long walks in the parks, talking girl talk, wearing matching bows in our hair, playing in the yard, getting all choked up over a chick flick. Yes, mother and daughter, friends at last. Yeah, like that's going to happen.

Murphy fit right into his new home; Py took a little longer, but eventually was accepted and even sat on Max's lap at night enjoying being part of the group. Unfortunately, one morning, six weeks to the day after mother died, Py died too. As I was fixing breakfast Pywacket acted like she had a hairball she couldn't cough up. This went on for about 30 minutes and Max took her to the vet, but before he could drive the five minutes home the vet called and said Py was having trouble breathing. They were trying to give her oxygen but couldn't get her to cooperate. As he was telling me what they were trying to do, he said he had to hang up. Within seconds he called back and said Py had died. He couldn't explain why and asked if I wanted to do an autopsy but I said no. What was the point? She was gone and nothing would bring her back. I like to think that Mother came for her. Several people have told me similar stories about pets dying soon after a loved one passed away. I think Mother worried so much about what would happen to Py that she came back for her, or maybe she loved her so much she couldn't bear to be without her; either way Py was gone and I felt guilty, like I had let Mom down. I vowed to take better care of Murphy.

I had so much death in such a short time that I didn't think I could bear anymore, but death was at my door and refused to go away. This time Weenie was the target. While caring for mother, dealing with Skeeter's death, Salem's death and finally Py's passing, I hadn't noticed Weenie had lost weight. In fact, he was half the size he normally was. How could I have not noticed? I took him to the vet and tests revealed he was diabetic. The prognosis was good; all I needed to do was give him medicine and two shots a day. Two shots a day, no way was that going to happen, and it was doubtful I'd be able to force medicine down him. Weenie was not the nurturing kind. It's not that I didn't want to. Hey, remember, I'm the woman who gave Salem enemas. But give Weenie a shot? That wasn't going to happen.

We had a decision to make; force Mr. Schizoid to endure unspeakable acts of horror, or let him go. Max and I wrestled with the problem daily. In the end I knew there was no way Weenie was going to let me play Nancy Nurse, but how could I live with the consequences? Boy, did I feel really, really sorry for myself. Life can be so shitty.

Right now there are two slots open at the Berry cat farm but there won't be for long. Knowing that nine is my lucky number, I'll keep a light in the window for those two furry creatures looking for shelter from the mean streets of Kansas.

Light Weaver Photography.

The cats, Max and me.